Robert Harbinson was born i[n] ... educated there and in Enniskille[n] ... ...[w]orked for a short time as a cabin boy on a dredger in Belfast Lough, then started training as a medical missionary. He left Belfast in 1944 to study theology at the South Wales Bible College and he went on to teach in north Devon, Canada and Venezuela. He took up diamond prospecting in Canada and South America and his hunting and trapping with the Blackfoot and Stony Indians began a long interest in American Indians who feature in his many travel books which were published in the 1960s under the name of Robin Bryans.

In more recent years he has become involved in music, concentrating on his work as an opera librettist from his London home/music studio.

Up Spake the Cabin Boy is the third volume of his four-part autobiography which begins with *No Surrender* and *Song of Erne* and ends with *The Protégé*. In addition to these and his travel books he has also published *Tattoo Lily and Other Ulster Stories*, the novel *Lucio*, and his collection of poems *Songs Out of Oriel*.

Up Spake the Cabin Boy

ROBERT HARBINSON

THE
BLACKSTAFF
PRESS
BELFAST AND WOLFEBORO, NEW HAMPSHIRE

First published in 1961 by
Faber and Faber Limited
This Blackstaff Press edition is a photolithographic facsimile
of the first edition printed by Latimer Trend & Company Limited

This edition published in 1988 by
The Blackstaff Press
3 Galway Park, Dundonald, Belfast BT16 0AN, Northern Ireland
and
27 South Main Street, Wolfeboro, New Hampshire 03894 USA
with the assistance of
The Arts Council of Northern Ireland

Printed by The Guernsey Press Limited

British Library Cataloguing in Publication Data
Harbinson, Robert, *1928-*
Up spake the cabin boy.
1. Northern Ireland. Harbinson, Robert –
Biographies
I. Title
941.6082'2'0924

Library of Congress Cataloging-in-Publication Data
Harbinson, Robert, 1928-
Up spake the cabin boy.
Reprint. Originally published: London : Faber and Faber, 1961.
Comprises the third part of the author's autobiography.
1. Harbinson, Robert, 1928-   — Biography — Youth.
2. Authors, Irish — 20th century — Biography.
3. Belfast (Northern Ireland) — Social life and customs.
I. Title.
PR6058.A617Z477   1988   828'.91409 [B]   88-4281
ISBN 0-85640-400-4

For

OZY

and

DAL

Contents

Local Terms

Barracks	Police station
Bachelor's buttons	Knapweed
Billy Boys	Protestants
Bour-tree	Elder
Ceili	An evening gathering
Chapel	Roman Catholic church
Codology	Tom-foolery
Creepies	Small stools
Cubs	Boys
Ditch	Dyke
Eegit	Idiot
Fenians	Roman Catholics
Hag-taper	Mullein
Inst	Royal Belfast Academical Institution
Island, the	Queen's Island
James the Fleeing	James II
Jinny	Effeminate person
King Billy	William III
Loanings	Lanes
Lough, the	Belfast Lough
Mickeys	Roman Catholics
Mitch school	Play truant

Local Terms

Pike of hay	Stack of hay
Ploughland	As much land as a plough could turn in a year
Purple charlies	Early purple orchids
Ruck	Rick
Sheugh	Ditch
Water, the	Irish Sea
Weasels	Stoats

CHAPTER I

The Coming of Black Tom

The day when Black Tom's boat entered Belfast our house knew no end of joy. For birthdays and Christmas we children had always been able to predict the presents and count the days. But Black Tom's leave ashore loomed all the greater in our calendar since it was a moveable feast, and consequently always one of surprise.

We never knew when, from anywhere in the whole wide world, he might land on our doorstep. And the marvel of things brought in his pockets! The oranges, the wooden clogs and shell dolls, and bottles of wine were utterly different from the usual sort of presents. One after the other he pulled them out, each devoured by our hungry eyes. The romance of distant places came right into our parlour. The dull Bible story-books and handkerchiefs which our great-aunts gave us at Christmas were not to be compared.

Often, we would still be sleeping, all huddled together in the big brass bed, when the unmistakable knock pounded on the door below. Like a flash, we were into our shifts and boots.

'Black Tom's come! Black Tom's come!' and down the stairs, breathless with excitement, to let in the returned seaman.

The Coming of Black Tom

My mother, Big 'Ina, had known him since she was fourteen. Soon after he had gone to sea they got engaged. But later during a spell of leave, they quarrelled so Big 'Ina went off and married my father. For years, Black Tom spent his leaves in the bars and cafés around the waterfront. Then he heard Big 'Ina was a widow with three kids. And there he was on the doorstep, his black, black hair well oiled and parted, his pockets bulging with good things for us children, his blue eyes beaming with undimmed admiration for Big 'Ina.

What stories of his travels he had to tell! What circuses, with clowns and everything, he took us to! What money he filled our fists with—the like of which we could not see again until his ship came home. For years, the big sallow-complexioned seaman was our favourite visitor. We thought him easily the best of my mother's boy-friends. There was of of course, another Tom after Big 'Ina. Tom the Grave-digger laid important claims for her favour. But the only thing we cared about him was that he played in a pipe-band, and wore a kilt and a great big busby made of fur with all sorts of plumes stuck in it. Knowing that no woman could resist a kilt, he usually stood at our door, resplendent in his regalia, after the heart-stirring twelfth of July ceremonies.

The 1939 War came, ringing more changes in our streets than ever the tinny Victorian church bells had done. I thought Black Tom the finest of all the war heroes, when his ship was blown up by a German torpedo. Everything went sky-high, and then came dreadfully down, to sink in the Atlantic's anonymous depths. All disappeared except Black Tom and some of the wreckage he clung to with an older man. Days passed before anyone found them drifting about like a matchbox in the gutter, among the desert of waves. We felt sorry that they had nothing to eat or drink while holding on to the floating bits of ship. Black Tom looked none-the-worse for it when we saw him afterwards. And how we enjoyed basking in the bright beams of his glory!

He reached the pinnacle of fame when the newspaper printed his photograph and told the story underneath. You could not ask for anything better than having your picture in the paper, we thought, except perhaps the king himself coming to pin on medals. The photograph was cut out and put in the frame of the kitchen mirror—a place of honour. In spite of appearances, Black Tom was injured, and in the end could not return to sea. Instead they gave him a good job down in the Island shipyard. And that is how he became a link in the chain of my life as well as in my mother's.

Black Tom had always promised Big 'Ina that he would 'see me right' in life and get me a good place in the Island. He meant it too. Now that my fourteenth birthday was behind me, I could no longer be an evacuee. The serious business of a 'trade' must begin. With desperate sadness at leaving County Fermanagh and the green paradise of the West, I prepared to turn from pine plantations and old woods to hulls and gantries, to tune my ears to rivetters' stuttering guns instead of twittering redpolls.

It was the Saturday after my return as an evacuee, and in walked Black Tom, He had come to stay until supper, bringing a bottle of 'port type'. There was to be no delay over my going to work. A job had already been fixed, starting Monday morning. Because of the war, a special permit to enter the Island docks must be obtained. Black Tom gave me a letter and I took it to the local barracks. Such an important errand demanded my new suit and bright claret tie. There could be absolutely no doubt now that I was a man—going like that for a pass into the Island.

Carefully stowing Black Tom's letter away so as not to crease it, I set out for the big, gloomy building. Not only did

I know the way, but remembered its inside, for I had been in there before. On that occasion, it had been against my will. Anybody could have seen that, by the way I kicked, screamed, and took vicious bites at the strong hands of the constable who had caught me stealing at the greengrocer's. However, no misgivings undermined my confidence when I went in for my pass. Apple-pinching days were long over.

All the same, it was a shock to find the identical sergeant inside. He knew me well. I had belonged to a bad gang along the railway, and might have done still if the war had not scattered us to the four winds. The sergeant showed no malice, but only surprise that I had grown nearly as tall as himself, in spite of only being fourteen. But this seemed an advanced age to me, and I considered he had no right in expecting to see the thin, pale-faced boy he had known before. In Fermanagh I lived the farmer's life, ate well, worked well, and was out in all weathers. Still, the policeman could hardly know this, and I accepted as kindly meant his comment about my 'having turned out well'. He handed me my pass, and hoped that I would 'keep a clean book'.

I did not go straight home, but called on the way at a man's shop. Feeling terribly important at being an Islandman, I ordered a pair of dungarees. In the parlour at home, wrapped up in brown paper, I already had a seaman's big jersey. Being home again was not without excitement, especially now I had come to a man's heritage. I would be getting my first wage-packet soon. Then the gates of plenty would open. In a flash, just as a drowning man is supposed to see a parade of his whole life, I saw the years behind me. On numberless occasions I had stood, nose pressed against shop-windows, looking at things that could not be mine. Now they would—some at least. I took a long time to get home, so that Black Tom and Big 'Ina were on the point of leaving. They were going for their

Saturday night fling. This took place down town, in the grand bars with late supper at Billy's fish parlour on the way back. They had left my tea on the table. Black Tom clapped me on the back and told me to meet him by the dock gate at seven o'clock on Monday morning.

Our house was crammed with lodgers. My mother could earn money more easily this way. Because of yet another operation, the doctors had forbidden her the heavier but more remunerative work in a munitions factory. But it was not long, in fact, before she did go back to handling the cold, shiny harvest of war. So some of the homeless war-workers in Belfast found themselves kipping in our little house. Room, of course, had to be made for me now. And I was to be treated just like the others though, naturally, there would be certain differences. For instance, I could not go out on a Saturday night booze-up like the other lodgers, who soon followed Black Tom and Big 'Ina out of the house.

I had a job to do on that Saturday. When the last one had gone and the house fell silent, I got the ink bottle and began a letter. It was to the Fermanagh farm people. I had been very sorrowful at parting, despite Belfast's glitter. The evacuation officer had put me on their farm, after I had been in and out of nine other billets in rapid succession. But somehow, the nine did not matter. Maggie and her elderly brother Christy had given me more than shelter, but a second home.

My pen seemed so inadequate for saying anything real to Maggie. Words in ink were poor substitute for all the fun we used to have. However, not to write was unthinkable. So I said that the journey home was good (was it? I had been numb with grief and hadn't noticed anything all the hundred miles from the West) and not that a piece of the 'posh' had been smashed. The 'posh' was a collection of china I had made during my stay at the farm. By any standards my collection

17

was big. To show Black Tom how much I approved of him, I had brought some of the china down from the tin trunk Maggie gave me. That Saturday, Big 'Ina's boy-friend had his fried tea out of Crown Derby plates and cups, that had once been used at the table of a country mansion in the West. Black Tom responded to this privilege graciously enough.

A brain-wave for Maggie's letter occurred to me. I would fill a page with drawings of all my favourite animals at the farm, put balloons in their mouths like the comics we read, and make them say amusing things. I worked hard at it, and feeling well-pleased with my handiwork, carefully printed the address on an envelope, and went out to the post. Too well I knew how and when the postman would go up the long lane to the farmhouse, and how Maggie would weep when she saw that the letter came from me.

How different my bed at home seemed from the one I had at the farm. And how different the night's noises—screaming trains instead of hooting owls, the hum of traffic instead of the susurrant wind in the trees. Partly because of that, and partly because thoughts of Monday morning excited me, I could not sleep. Would Black Tom come back to stay the night, I wondered? For things were not as they used to be. Big 'Ina had another permanent boy-friend now on the railway.

Then, without noticing, I fell asleep and did not wake until the light of a clear Sunday streamed in. Although I had come home again—home to the streets whose corners were punctuated by church steeples, pubs and pawnbrokers, this for me was no ordinary Belfast Sunday. In living memory, there had been no other Sunday when I had not to get up and go to innumerable services in the parish church. But we children were no longer parish orphans and obliged to attend. We were grown up now—was I not tomorrow to enter the dock gates with thanksgiving? So we turned our backs on the church, flauntingly and finally. For years we all had to mind our p's and q's, during the week as well as on Sunday, and Big 'Ina as well as ourselves. And this was all for fear we would lose our income from the poor-box. Now that the economic pressure was relieved, we brazenly thrust off our ecclesiastical guardians. Many the time we had thought of them as oppressors. Now, my mother openly passed the Rector in the street completely ignoring him. But I always spoke to Ould Willie. Some said Big 'Ina behaved like that because of the boy-friends and the Rector's disapproval. To me he had always been a kind, if stern, figure in my childhood.

Nevertheless, I did not go on that Sunday morning to the pseudo-Gothic church round the corner. Big 'Ina was against it. Instead I packed up some sandwiches and went up to the city cemetery. Sordid acres of it straggled at the foot of the mountain. How well it came back to me as I approached the iron gates—gates that had such an air of finality about them. For Sunday morning they were open wide as though a public park lay beyond them. Near these gates, in order to be first out at the Resurrection, the wealthy had been buried. Some slept under ten-foot columns topped with marble drapery and marble Greek urns. Swan-limbed angels, also of white marble, hovered over others. The lives of some of the rich merchants had been selfish enough to petrify any guardian angel.

Yes, I recalled the place. Two years in the country had not cured me of that. The high obelisks and miniature church towers put up sixty years before, were not likely to have crumbled. I hurried by them, pausing no more on the way to my destination than to refresh my mind, and to imprint their grotesque forms again on my inner eye.

The acres of the rich gave way eventually to the acres of

the poor. Here the ground was not so weighed down, not so gloomy with granite. Not far now, and I would pass little Molly's grave. She had been one of my favourite girls and had walked to school with me. The only thing I could find of her now was an open book, done in bloodless marble. Written on its pallid pages was the bald fact that Molly had died aged 10 years 3 months. Well, I had escaped *that*. Without doubt Molly had looked more like an angel as she lay silent and waxy in her coffin, than the swanky, swan-limbed ones fluttering down the hill. It was a strange coincidence for me to stop by that grave on a Sunday morning. The last time Molly and I walked together had been on our way to morning Sunday School. Molly wore a short dress almost up to her buff, and some corner-boys laughed at her. She rounded on them indignantly and retaliated with an old jingle,

> *Ahem! Ahem!*
> *I'm not ashamed of my shirt,*
> *My mother sent me out to church,*
> *And told me not to play with dirt.*

And after Molly, on to the rows of wooden crosses marking the graves of soldiers and sailors who had already died in the war. Was that all they would get? I was coming closer to the mountain now, and the poorer section of the cemetery. At least, here you could see the ground, for the headstones, if any, were only tiny. Those graves with none, made do with little marble doves set on the grassy mounds.

Then I came to the one row I had loved better than all the others. My father's grave was here.

In bygone years people used to tell me I was 'the spit of my ould da'. The neighbours said this nostalgically, reminding themselves and me of the young window-cleaner. The great-aunts, whom I hated, used it as a term of scorn. They regarded my mother meeting my father as the worst match, the worst mistake in the whole family history. But even my mother and elder sister used the term against me, when I fought and carried on at home. That my poor father had been fond of the bottle there was no denying. His nightly home-coming had been heard with dread in the deserted street. When people called me his 'spit' they meant not only in looks, but ways too. Like him, I had also mitched school, and turned quite wild, following him in his tracks.

I cared for nothing and nobody, no not I. Only one thing in life I cherished and that was my father's memory. Because I was only six the day he was buried, I had not got many memories. But such as there were, I kept fiercely inviolate from the sneers of others. Moreover, I had not seen him laid out in his coffin as I had other relatives and neighbours, well before I reached six years. The great-aunts forbade it. Ever afterwards I hated them for that.

My mother told us what the doctor from the asylum said about him (he had fallen while cleaning some upper windows when twenty-seven years old, and the spike of a garden railing went through his brain). The doctor said it when Big 'Ina went to see his corpse—'Robbie was like a lad of sixteen'. This gave me no end of painful pleasure. Pleasure because I thought my father must have looked very beautiful for the doctor to have said what he did, and pain because I was not allowed to see that stark beauty.

As the great-aunts died one by one, dropping like flies from a ceiling, we children had been to see them lying, not un-comically, in their grave-clothes. We were even made to kiss the hard lips that could say no more cruel things to us. But because my father drank and gambled and was not, would not, and some said could not, be 'saved', we had been barred from seeing him.

The Coming of Black Tom

For that above all I hated them, and for years wanted to put the omission right. The rich, I knew, had vaults like rooms where their loved ones were put on slabs like food on larder shelves. I imagined they were always going to have a look at the dead. My decision to rectify the great-aunts' cruelty, caused one of my earliest bouts of 'trouble'. I got some boards from somewhere in the cemetery and cunningly made a platform, over one-half of the grave. Some stone wreaths of flowers covered with huge glass cheese-lids went on top of the boards, making an excellent camouflage. From underneath, bit by bit, day by day, I removed little oatmeal sacks of soil, with as much skill as, later, war-prisoners in Germany used when escaping. I emptied my little sacks on the heaps of earth by new graves. I had made a fine hole, before it was discovered to the authorities' horror. Nobody understood.

Such thoughts, and a thousand other memories of the hours I had spent by the grave, flooded in on me, as I walked towards it that Sunday morning in a bright July. But as I looked down on the forsaken grave, changed because nobody had tended it during my two years away, I knew that I too had changed. And the simple plot, the single-human-size grave that once had been my all in life, meant nothing to me any more. Its hold over me was gone.

Perhaps the love I had found in Fermanagh had dissolved the bitterness that drove me to the cemetery. Now that I had come home to Belfast again, my father's grave seemed, somehow, irrelevant. But not my father himself. It had been like that before, on the occasions when I thought my father was still alive. Perhaps his madness might have been so complete that we had been told of his death by the great-aunts, to wipe his 'evil' existence from our minds. At times, this seemed the only explanation of events, for why had my sisters and me never seen the evidence of his death, the body?

The Coming of Black Tom

It was absurd to hide him from us in that way. We could not possibly have been frightened, because he had lived in the house with us for months, before going away. His wounded head and shattered limbs caused him to shout and rave if anyone went near to wash him. But he had called for me in bed, during the last delirium before the asylum, and I had nestled amongst the plaster-of-paris casing, and scratched his back for him.

I suppose a sigh, or something very like it, must have escaped me, as I stood again by the place that no longer absorbed my emotions. My father's back, I knew, no longer required scratching because the plaster made him sweat—even though the sun fell with powerful strokes amongst the cypresses. Although his death was tragic for me, I had never thought of it as being so for him. So many of his friends died young. In the next grave five children had been buried, and all were under twelve years old. For many years, I had expected to be the next.

Yet tomorrow I was going with a country-tanned face to the Island.

An impulse seized me to get out of the cemetery as quickly as possible, and go away up the mountain behind it. That high hill loomed as an auspicious symbol of hope for the imminent future. I stayed long enough to clear the grave of its matted weeds, and to put the little stone dove on his feet. Then I hurried out by a side gate, near the poor walled-up Jews, buried so secretly and separately, and turned to the mountain.

My new Belfast life might touch the old one at many points, but not as far as the cemetery was concerned. I would visit it, naturally, but not haunt it. As if in compensation, my love for my father, I realized, would have to show itself in pride and defence of his memory. This was because of Harry.

The Coming of Black Tom

Harry was my mother's boy-friend, her steady now for six years. Greater, darker, and more terrible than the shadow of the fifteen great-aunts (my maternal grandmother's sisters) in my life, was that cast by Harry.

None of us could forget the day he walked into our lives— a Saturday. Crowds on their way to the matches at the football stadium poured along the entry at the back of our house, as a short cut. Any washing hung up to dry in the alleyway was taken down, and even the clothes-lines removed for safety. Neighbours locked the back gates, between yard and entry. No public conveniences existed for miles around, and should the gates be ajar, football fans would push in to use the yard lavatories.

Our own gate could not be fastened because the lock had been broken off long ago. The door itself had once been kicked off when one of us children tried to get in after being locked out. A new door duly arrived, but its bolt did not long survive our rough usage. In the end, we resorted to pushing the dust-bin against it, to keep dogs and other leg-lifters out of the yard. On Saturdays our bin proved particularly ineffectual, as the men emptied it on Fridays. It was too light to keep either man or beast out for long, let alone rats from the adjoining railway line.

During this particular Saturday afternoon, we saw our boltless door swing on its one good hinge and a figure dash into the lavatory. My sisters and I, and a neighbour who had called in, watched to see who it could be. Of course, the lavatory door had no lock or bolt either. It only had four small holes drilled near the top to let light in—provided you were sufficiently fussy in wanting to push the door to. Curious more than anxious, we waited to see what stranger we had entertained unawares. But after what we considered an interval long enough to meet normal demands, he still made no appearance. Curiosity changed to concern, and then into laughter. It must be diarrhoea, we concluded. He made no move and we went into the yard, calling for him to come out.

When Harry did come out, it was not to flee into the alley-way again, as others before him had done. Instead, he came into our parlour, and sat conjuring with pennies. They disappeared in a trice down his sleeve, and then, bold as brass, he plucked them out again from amongst his thick golden curls. That was clever for you! I had never known a man to have such beautiful hair, nor so curly. I teased him with,

> *Curly head the barber*
> *Stole a lump of beef,*
> *He stuffed it up his shaving skirt*
> *And called himself a thief.*

He grew tired of tricks before we did, and produced a big, hooked pipe. From it he sent up aromatic trails of smoke, with a flavour that became a familiar smell about the house.

At first we all liked Harry. He was good-looking and jolly. After his visits we always found half a dozen stout bottles, waiting to be returned at a halfpenny rebate each. It was understood that, 'Uncle' Harry as we called him, would never become the wonderful new daddy we were always imploring Big 'Ina to find us. Harry already possessed a wife and family. This constituted a difficulty because being parish orphans, our lives were dominated by the church. Not a breath of scandal would be countenanced by the Rector. So Harry had to be kept a secret. He came on Saturdays, mingling unobserved with the football crowds, or at night, when only the most adventurous of lovers loitered in the entry.

Where true love is, obstacles enhance rather than diminish the romance. Despite the existing wife and church ordinances, my mother and Harry were happy enough as the years went by. Black Tom's calls were not so frequent as to cause any disturbance. But it proved, in practice, very difficult to keep Harry a secret. He worked as an engine-driver on the railway. Before passing our house he always let out an enormous blast of his whistle, so that Big 'Ina could be at the window in time to wave. Sometimes when he drove the slow goods-train on the track next to the back door, he would stop the engine and give a message across the paling. And a steam-engine with forty wagons behind, hissing and creaking at one's back door is difficult to hide, especially near a long row of houses.

My own regard for Harry did not persist like Big 'Ina's did. On the opposite side of his railway line from our house ran a wide verge thick with sally-bushes. Here lay the principal haunt of the boys' gang I joined. My crimes against humanity met with every kind of reaction from Big 'Ina's strap to the great-aunts' shocked horror. But that had been in the family, and quite private. But my crimes now became public. The police were always after the gang, but we were generally too nimble for them. And Harry, no doubt with the finest intentions, tried to put a stop to my bad ways. I revolted, and enmity was born between us.

Deep, deep within me, I probably hated his attempt to usurp my father's place. As time went on, I found my dislike more and more justifiable. It satisfied some inner craving. The superficial causes of my dislike were simple enough—his telling me off for risking 'trouble' with the gang, or his taking the empty stout bottles back himself. At that time, too, I had approached a very early puberty, and its emotional disturbances found a ready outlet in my anti-Harry attitude.

The bad people of this world are often blamed for crimes they do not commit. Nobody believes their protestations of innocence. And so I copped it one day while playing in the street outside our house. A woman came to the door and asked for Harry. In innocence I asked if it might be *our* 'Uncle' Harry she wanted? The very man apparently. To her repeated loud knockings with our knocker, no answer came. This was strange for I knew my mother to be in. Pushing the visitor aside, I yelled through the letter-box that a woman wanted to see Big 'Ina. I made such a noise that my mother did eventually fly out of the house, in a towering rage. The woman was none other than Harry's wife. Inadvertently, I had told everything.

As I climbed up towards the mountain on that first Belfast Sunday after my return, I realized that there at least was one situation unchanged. If anything, Harry was more firmly entrenched than ever. Now that the apron-strings of parish charity no longer tied our family, Harry could openly come and go as he pleased. He had his own key to the door. On arriving home, I had noticed immediately that my father's photograph in the parlour had been taken out of its frame, and Harry's put in. Before going to bed, I had found the brown picture, and all the other personal things of my father's, and locked them safely away with my 'posh'. Now that I was to all intents another man come into the house, all would surely not be well.

Climbing and panting, at last I reached the mountain top. For a few more hours I could pretend that freedom was still mine, that this was the country, and that in my house no strained atmosphere prevailed. I could not see how they regarded me—as an awkward adolescent with large hands and even larger feet.

The July day had now ascended to its glory. I lay down, basking in the heat among purple clover that contrasted with the bright, nutty whin bushes. By leaning on one elbow, I had a view over the whole city. Right across its stones, I could see to where the broad Lough ended in a flickering asp's tongue of river, silver amongst the dun mud flats. Church spires and stalky chimney stacks stood stark in the warm air, glowering over the mean streets clustered about them in monotonous rows. Belfast was a city at war, so its chimneys still belched into the Sabbath babble of prayers.

Nearer to me than most of the sprawling city, now streaky with light and shade from the cotton-wool trails of smoke that cut off the sun here and there, stood a Catholic chapel. In this chapel the people had their throats blessed by a lighted candle, to save them from choking on fish-bones. War had silenced the city's bells. But so often before I went away to the country, I had wondered why our Protestant preachers ranted against the Catholics ringing their meagre bells, when our own steeples confused the air with clanging carillons. Now I knew, for I had lived among Mickeys in Fermanagh and had seen their altar bells.

From my high mountain seat I could see our own parish church. On how many such mornings had I been under its roof at that hour. I knew well enough that about now was the time when most of the congregation left the morning service, so that the specially devout might take Holy Communion. This rite was particularly puzzling to us children, who were allowed into all services but this. What went on inside when the vast red curtains were drawn on their brass rings by the sexton who forbade us even to peep? Somebody said that the people inside even indulged in such a popish practice as to kneel when the body was cut up.

How long ago it all seemed, and how Fermanagh had altered me.

And then my thoughts wandered from the city's churches to the cathedrals of gantries on Queen's Island, outlined like fine tracery of steel against the docks. I had come home. Tomorrow I would show my pass and be through the mysterious portals into manhood—an Islandman indeed.

Fine as those gantry aisles might be, I was not an enthusiastic acolyte. My heart was still roaming the green loamings of Fermanagh.

CHAPTER II

Five-a-Bed

In all the years of my childhood, my mother had never taken a tram to work—except coming home on Friday with the pay packet. And even then she alighted at the penny fare-stage half a mile from our house. What revolutions the war caused in our life. Now, even my younger sister, on going to pay the furniture instalment, took a tram right to the stop nearest the top of our street.

I too, on my first Monday morning as a working man, went to catch a tram.

It was early enough for me to get the workers' cheap fare. Not that I needed to, for I was going to earn exactly twice as much for myself as four years previously my mother had been earning. And she had to keep the whole family on her wage. I needed no early call. Long before five o'clock I lay awake. When I did get up, I allowed more than enough time to cut my midday 'piece', and put on the new dungarees. They were stiff, the buttons would hardly fasten, and the cloth smelt like a mixture of glue and mothballs. Then, making sure that my mother could not see, I took a lump of margarine and greased my hair. I considered this the essence of good grooming. Unlike brilliantine, it had a thick consistency and plastered my hair back like seal-fur in the water. The trick

had not been learnt recently. Years before, at the holiday
home for boys in County Down where I went in summer,
everyone had used margarine for this.

The ring of my hob-nailed boots followed me up the
street, and friendly nods greeted me at the tram stop. I had
forgotten how friendly the Belfast people could be, even at
six o'clock in the morning. 'Great weather for ducks,' they
would remark, or 'There's divil-the-hate in the paper
today.'

On succeeding mornings I found the same people waiting
for the same tram. Their complete submission to the harsh
dictates of the shipyards faintly shocked me. Though friendly,
the pale faces looked as if a light inside the men had long ago
been extinguished. Getting up to greet the sun on hayfields,
and to see the last of the night mist chased away from the
meadows, was a different thing. In Fermanagh people got up
early, but to a day which held at least the promise of some fine
thing. The men waiting for the tram seemed doomed to a
gloomy world of metal, where no birds would sing nor
brooks flow. And they accepted it. Standing behind each
other, they were indistinguishable in their black clothes from
the man in front and the one behind.

At last the tram came and we all filed in. Whatever the
weather, I made for the upstairs. At each end a kind of little
balcony projected which only had an iron railing. I sat there,
the breeze blowing in my face, enjoying this rocking over the
street below. I got an indefinable thrill from this, a habit left
over from the very rare days in childhood when we rode
trams.

Gradually, I came to know the men though they talked
about little except dogs and football and the weather. They
joked and ragged each other, and particularly me at first. You
might have thought the early workers' tram quite hilarious as

it lumbered along, grinding over its lines. But it depressed me. It may have been the colourless faces, and the drab clothes soaked in evil-smelling grease that not a hundred washings could ever remove. Some of the men wore white mufflers knotted curiously across their dark Oxford shirts like St. Andrew's crosses. All had cloth caps. I also owned a cap, a big, old-fashioned one, made of large segments sewn together. It looked like a cake cut into wedges ready for eating. I had been so proud of my cap in Fermanagh. But I soon realized it was a country effort, and took it off, and wrapped it round my 'piece' parcel.

On the first Monday, I arrived at the dock gates long before Black Tom appeared. Eventually I spotted him amongst the crowds, and we were soon through the gates. Tom nodded at the police standing guard. They did not even ask to see my brand-new pass. Half-disappointed, I followed Tom. It was still so early that the ground shone with mist that clung around dim shapes. We walked as though through a forest whose trees were made of steel, harshly etched against the morning sky. Instead of leaf-laden branches reaching out to catch the sun's rays, I saw a multitude of cranes, swinging poles, and a phalanx of gantries. Tom was hurrying, weaving his way quickly between other men, anonymous and hurrying. Vastness threatened to engulf me. I had made no reckoning as to the size of everything on the Island. A rush of loneliness caught me and I felt dreadfully homesick for the farm. What would I not have given to be back in those quiet ploughlands again.

Then I got a sniff of the sea, and my love of ships suddenly returned. How could I have forgotten a recurrent ambition of my old life so easily? The unfulfilled longings returned then, the numberless times I had stood at quaysides aching to go to sea. Now the shipyards brought it back, but stronger. Boats and bits of boats and hulks of boats were everywhere. The gantry forest touched the sky because of boats, and all the men came on the early trams because of boats. Our sort lived and died because of boats. In remembered excitement, my homesickness vanished.

Many of the ships were wounded veterans of war, grey and remorseful in the filtering light. Alongside, the skeleton hulls of Harland and Wolff's bays stuck up, like the bones of washed-up whales. The incessant chatter of automatic hammers echoed in their bowels, and sparks flew out where the riveters worked in the dim, smoky recesses. Trails of cloud flung up from the sea into a ragged sky, the cry of twisted metal, and the sight of men sweating in the cavernous holds, sent a shudder through me. Hardly daring to pause lest I lose sight of Black Tom, I scurried in the terrifying din under the mammoth cradles to the quay.

Now I could see the harbour, and the greasy water lapping against the wall. The mist was dissolving under the climbing sun. Tugs nosed busily in and out, between liners and cargo-boats well down in the water with heavy loads, and filthy colliers and tightly-packed cross-channel steamers. The wind blowing from the water brought the desperate wail of hooters, and the crying of gulls.

Then Black Tom stopped abruptly. Inside a wooden hut belonging to my employers, he handed me over to a clerk, and promptly left. I felt like a parcel that had been delivered. After Black Tom's exit, the young man swivelled on his high stool again to finish adding a column of figures. I seemed to be of no consequence to him whatsoever. He muttered like a witch over a cauldron as he checked and rechecked entries in his book. He fingered his hair in nervous agitation and kept adjusting thick-lensed, horn-rimmed glasses, which threatened to pull his ears off. He varied this by biting the top of his pencil until it looked like a chewed cinnamon stick, or by stuffing a finger up his nose. A clock on the wooden wall, far too large for the little hut, ticked loudly. I thought I had been out of bed for hours.

All kinds of disquieting ideas raced through my mind. Was I to work for this sallow-faced, puffy-fleshed young man? Because I had not reached the regulation age for beginning an engineering apprenticeship, other work had to be found meanwhile for me. I already knew it might be something of the message-boy type. But if it was to be no more than waiting around for this humourless creature on his high stool, then my chances of excitement on the Island looked very thin. Would I have to board that tram every morning, just to spend my days running to and from the little clock-loud hut? Surely Black Tom had not let me in for such a life.

Another stool stood near me, but I dare not sit down, for fear the clerk should turn round and demand haughtily who I thought I was. It would never do to let Black Tom down, for the young man had an important air about him.

At last the hut door opened and a stout little man came in. The clerk swivelled on his high stool again, pointed to me, and swivelled back. He could not speak, otherwise the figures poised in his silently-moving lips would be lost on the air, and he would have to go to the top of the column again. The little man collected me, and I learned my fate. A message-boy I would certainly be, but not a common longshoreman who rode a bicycle over the cobbled streets. Most of the time, I would be going out to a whole series of dredgers, tugs, barges, launches, and mysterious boats far out to sea. These ships reclaimed the shallow verges of the Lough with mud cleared from the constantly silting harbour and channels. As the little man explained all this to me, my spirits rose again. In all possibility I would never see the young man in the wooden hut again. No clerking for me. I was going to be a real sailor after all!

The man besides being short was also fat, and a Scot. More than that, he was the Bursar, and I was to be under him.

Belying the slowness suggested by his rotundity the Bursar scurried along, talking all the time. He did not always look directly at me as he spoke, but kept turning his head, and darting his eyes all over the place. Very little of what was going on escaped him. He carried a shiny suitcase, and gave me a canvas bag to carry inside a large but not-so-smart case. Our first job together was to go shopping. Before we left the docks by the same gate I had entered not an hour before, Bursie pointed out the dredger whose urgently-needed groceries I was to deliver.

Great bundles of ration books filled half of Bursie's shiny case. My first lesson from him concerned the care of the garter. This held the ration books together. When taking it off, I must always slip it on to my wrist like a bangle. Never on any account must the garter be left thoughtlessly behind on shop counters, a crime so often committed by my careless predecessors. Thus forewarned I went with him into the shops where he commanded not only respectful attention, but a kind of allegiance. Bursie, quite clearly, stood no nonsense where his business was concerned.

I coped successfully with the ration books, and manipulated the all-important garter. Then Bursie left me, to attend to other ships, and I had to struggle back to the docks with a heavy load of provisions. It strained at the handle of the large suitcase, and even threatened to tear the cord in the sailor's canvas bag from its moorings. The only thing which impressed me among this load was the prunes. What my mother would not have given for a fraction from the bags of prunes I carried! Because of the war, nobody had got sight of a prune for years. I could not have felt more important with bullion in the bags. But prunes, apparently, were just a routine part of the life I was to lead.

On the way back to the dock gates, I wondered how I would manage to get my pass out for the policeman, without dropping the precious stores. However, I sailed through by a nod, as with Black Tom earlier. How the guard could distinguish between the featureless figures in their grimy overalls and caps, which all looked alike, I failed to understand. Perhaps somebody had slipped word to him, that I was the prune-carrier and practically a V.I.P.

Since seven o'clock, the docks had changed appearance. The towering structures of half-built hulls in their cradles, and the soaring cranes and gantries, seemed just a shade less terrifying. After all, I thought, picking my way insignificantly beneath them, I *was* a sailor. With no difficulty I traced my way through the docks, and reached the place where a green, slimy incline slid into the water, banking the shore. There lay the dredger whose food I carried. The ferryman did not hear my call. No wonder, the dredger's noise drowned everything else. Like monsters coming up from the depths, bucket after bucket broke surface. With demoniac clanking, and a fine cascade of water spewing out, they soared high up on the chain belt, tipped over depositing their mud on the noisy chute. Then, bottoms up, without the slightest sign of hurry, they returned to the harbour-bed again.

By sheer luck the ferryman saw me, and came to collect me. Quite near inshore, a huge ship gleamed white in the sun, and our creaking bumboat took us under its radiant superstructure. Some of the crew leaning over her rail far above our heads, threw spicy remarks at the ferryman. He did not take much notice, for he was too busy, working our single oar furiously to and fro. I sat in the sheets with the suitcase, and he stood in the stern, paddling like a Venetian gondolier.

Before I climbed aboard the dredger, the ferryman had to know everything contained in the case and the canvas bag. He even filched a handful of prunes before starting back. But then, I could hardly object, as I had already stopped several times to sample the prunes myself.

The boatman spoke with a strong Free State accent, and called the prunes 'quick shifters'. It was the first of many such names I was to hear given to food or people and ships. Though seldom polite these local terms were always pertinent and witty, summing up a situation or character. Indeed, before we reached the dredger, the fine, white ship beside us had lost all glamour for me.

'What is it?' I asked in innocence. Often, in years gone by, I had viewed this gleaming symbol from a distant quay.

'Gordam Clap Palais,' the ferryman replied unconcernedly. I would often see in the days ahead, this floating sewage farm go away out into the Channel to excuse her excuses.

The sea, like the country, is rarely romantic for those whose livelihood comes from it. Aboard the dredger, I had no time for idle dreaming about being a sailor. Although Bursie, to whom I was responsible, did not come back for a long time, nevertheless, my services were put to good use. Piles of potatoes needed scraping, piles of plates and mugs wanted to be washed. Scruffily-written notes had to be collected from the men for delivery ashore, as well as money for personal shopping. There were dredgers and reclaimers anchored far out, whose crews seldom went on land. So in the following weeks I had to buy a motley of things for them, from razor-blades and Johnson's Baby Powder to ear-rings and toys for their families. And I never made a trip back into Belfast when a visit to the Post Office was not included. I always stood at the counter a long time, as the men asked me endlessly for postal orders, which went off to their homes or the football pools.

I became so involved with potatoes and pots on that first morning, that when Bursie turned up on the bank, he had to caper about to call me. The irascible Scot found further fault in my manhandling of the little boat, for it was I who had to row from the dredger and pick him up. But at last I got him back without a ducking. Rowing became an every day experience, to be thought no more about than catching the early morning tram. Before long, I could even stand up and do the pudding-stirring, single-oar rowing. That Monday also taught me another art. The first bucket of kitchen waste I threw overboard went into the wind, and returned, not on the water like Solomon's bread, but in a mess against the hull. Fortunately, nobody who mattered saw it. I knew then the proper side for waste disposal was the leeward, away from prank-playing breezes—the side in fact, used by the more experienced men when they baptized the Lough waters.

Had there been time for reflection, I might have pondered the wonder of time—how slowly each minute had dragged reluctantly by when I stood in the clerk's wooden office, and how swiftly whole hours sped by once I got aboard. I did not even think about Fermanagh and the farm for more than the briefest of moments. There was enough to keep me busy the whole day through. I might be in the middle of penning a letter for a bargee to his wife, when a cry of 'Five-a-bed' would reach me.

The cry meant that I must start to serve out the inevitable prunes. It seemed the men could not keep fit without them. The whole operation was a system of mass-production. Rows of dishes lined the table like parts on a factory's moving belt. In each, a controlled amount of bright canary custard was emptied, falling in thick folds like blankets. Then from a can, I had to place five of the 'quick shifters' into each dish—'five-a-bed'. This job did not entirely lack its own special fascination. I could study the curious phenomenon of prune sinking into custard, seeing it perhaps as a sea-creature being sucked under by a sea-anemone. There could be races also between dishes, to see whose prunes went under first. Diversions of this kind depended, naturally enough, on the pressure of other things requiring my attention. I had to be as careful as a bank cashier counting notes. There would be trouble if any man found less than five prunes in his dish. But that was mild compared with the abuse I got from Cook, should he find six stones in the empty bed!

I never knew, as I rattled on the early tram from home to Island, how my day would begin. Some new situation always presented itself. For all I could guess, I might be despatched to deliver prunes to the moon. Even the time varied. At almost pre-dawn there might be a launch full of workers whom I joined on their way to a distant dredger. For a seven o'clock breakfast aboard, I might have to deliver fish. And often my pockets were heavy with money that must be put in the Post Office Savings for the men, or oddments they wanted from the shops before I went to the docks.

After the Post Office, my next most frequent port-of-call was the chemist's. Taddy's photographs took me there more than any other single item. Taddy was a deck-hand on one of the tugs. He could be a Vesuvius ready to erupt over me, should I fail to bring his requirements because of war-time shortages. But he was my great friend also. What he lacked in height, he made up in muscle that lay like hunks of meat from his thick bull-neck, down a fabulous torso, to beefy thighs as hard as iron. Unfortunately his super-development trailed away below his knees, ending in comparatively spindly ankles. His appearance was undoubtedly that of a tadpole, his disproportionate namesake.

Taddy slopped lazily about the tug in thick wellingtons. He wore these turned down at the top, so the thinness of the shank beneath was concealed. The thighs, his biceps and shoulders fairly bursting out of a blue roll-neck jersey, needed no deceit. Taddy was not in ignorance of his physique, in fact it caused him no end of pride and pleasure—hence my frequent trips to the photography counter at the chemist's. Whenever opportunity presented itself, and sometimes when it did not, Taddy would strip and emerge in small, blue swimming slips. He must have been about nineteen, and was I knew, anxious to get himself featured in physical culture magazines. He thrust a camera into my hands, and stood flexing his impossible muscles, expanding his pectorals, sucking in his already-flat stomach. From nowhere, he produced two flanges of muscle on his back, that sprang out and from the camera's viewpoint made him look like a cobra with distended hood.

Black clouds obscured the smiling blue of our friendship if the photos turned out badly. Heaven help me, should I have ruined them by moving the camera. He could not bear to have the sculpture of his muscles blurred. It never occured to me then to wonder why, apart from the magazines, Taddy cultivated his body beyond the point of normal fitness or ability. But he was my friend, the nearest to me in age, and we got on well together. Because he seldom went ashore during the day, and so looked forward to the things brought, I always took care over his requirements. Sometimes he would bargain for my shoes or my watch, or some other coveted thing newly acquired with my wages. Being of quite an opposite build from him, such bartering was seldom successful, though when it was, he always gave me the better part. Like all the men, Taddy was generous.

Carrying the men's money perhaps placed an unfair responsibility on me. But I would take no chances. I made a cloth bag with long strings, so that I could tie it round my body. This kept the money safe, not only on my way home but also during the night. Because our house was chock-a-block with lodgers, including several Islandmen, I had to share my room with two others. During the course of weeks a couple of rogues came and went, but none tried to fiddle with my money-bag in the night.

The men's money, however, was not the only money I had. From Fermanagh I had returned with a large sum in my savings account, earned from my winter trapping and the sale of fruit that burgeoned Maggie's gardens and orchards. A burning ambition seized me to turn this into a complete hundred pounds. Who in our family had ever owned such riches? Nobody except the great-aunts. My father married and set up house on £25. I gave half of my weekly pay-packet to my mother, the rest went to the Post Office. An exception to this golden rule had to be made with my very first wage-packet. To be a complete man, a hat was essential. It would certainly help to conceal my big nose, and balance other adolescent abnormalities. Long ago I had decided what kind of a hat it would be. In Fermanagh, I had seen 'the quality' out shooting pheasants. One young toff wore a green soft hat, whose chief glory was its stitching. All across it, the stitches went in criss-cross pattern, light grey on the green felt like young corn, hairy in the spring furrows.

But the buying of the hat taught me much about myself. It amounted to a revelation. For a start, I never realized I had such a large head. Its profile, front and back, was a shock to me. Yet worse things showed themselves in the shop's mirrors, cunningly hinged to present the customer, Picasso-like, with a score of faces simultaneously. I sickened, quite suddenly, for I could see all the evidence of Divine wrath, making a delayed but fatal appearance in my too-worldly flesh. I once had a tendency to stoop. But plainly, this had now grown into a hump. Horror-stricken, I gazed in dismay into the endless perspective of the mirrors. The figure standing there was, undeniably, a hunchback. The hat, which a shop assistant put into a scrunching paper bag, became nothing. As he stood by the door to show me out (it had been quite an expensive hat) I felt he was ushering me into outer darkness.

Of all the religious maxims branded into my soul during childhood, none burnt deeper than *Be sure your sin will find you out*. Now God had found me out, and had started an ugly hump growing on me. How could I have been so rash, as to turn my back on the church, because I was no longer a parish orphan? I might have known God would get His own back.

Obviously, this punishment had been selected for me with more than a special skill. For when I had been about six years old, I had joined in with other children of the neighbourhood in tormenting the crippled mute. He had stood every day on the railway bridge, watching the passing trains beneath him with a fearful eye. As he materialized out of the plumes of engine smoke, we imagined him as a monster. We shouted wicked things at him, and ran as near as we dared knowing he could never catch us because of his bad legs.

Hearing of this behaviour, Big 'Ina severely reprimanded me, and concluded the scolding with an assurance that I would be transformed into such a thing myself if I mocked the deaf mute. I only half believed her. Yet soon after, when I went to stay with a great-aunt because Big 'Ina was in hospital, I had to spend painful hours prone on the floor because, said great-aunt, *I was developing a stoop*. And Divine vengeance pursued me into the country when I escaped from Belfast as an evacuee. Into our classroom one morning walked the Rector. He came straight to where I sat, and handed me a pair of dumb-bells, telling me to straighten up. The blood rushed to my ears, guilt flooded my mind.

I had not expected God's stern judgement to chase me as I fled across the borders of childhood into manhood. My heart thumped in front of those mirrors in the hat shop, for they told me that my hump was growing as big as the mute's. When I got home, I put the hat on top of the wardrobe among other unwanted things. I spent hours on my knees during the days that followed, praying to the pound-of-flesh God in whom we believed. 'Please God take it away', I repeated endlessly, wanting my knees to hurt so that the Deity would see I was earnestly repentant for having mocked the mute. At night, my fear penetrated even the sound sleep that a day's work in the keen Lough air could bring. Fully awake, I would wonder for a moment, for what purpose I had woken. Then awful remembrance of the hump returned. I jumped out of bed to begin the feverish praying again, 'Please God, take it away.' Naturally prayers must be said out of bed—God took no notice of sluggards who mumbled them between the sheets. The lodgers in the same room were astonished at this, should they still be awake at two or three in the morning. But they probably thought it was the first symptom of the religious mania I developed later.

I did exercises and lay on the floor for hours just gazing at the ceiling, before the Lord spoke. Solely to please Him, I had even begun to read the Bible right through from the start. Not until I reached the Book of Proverbs, however, did I hear the 'still small voice'. To what else could the words in chapter thirty-one refer but my hump? I read them avidly, and then re-read them, *She girdeth her loins with strength, and strengtheneth her arms.*

I was not altogether sure what part of the body loins might be. In fact, I did not know at all. But the Book made it perfectly plain that I had to get girded up. Next day, I made opportunity, for inspiration from the Bible was not to be treated lightly. While in the city on a dozen errands, I slipped into Smithfield Market. I hunted along the rows of stalls in the covered alleys and in the dim shops behind them. At last I found it, a lengthy wireless aerial. I could not even stop to bargain for it, as I had always done with oddments I bought there.

At home that night, I girded up my protuberant shoulder-blades in no uncertain fashion. When the whole wire was criss-crossed and finally fastened, I could hardly move. What with my money-bag tied round my stomach and the wireless aerial all over my chest, I was a curious bed-fellow for the lodgers. But they gained no glimpse of the loin-girding, for I kept my shirt on in bed. Anxious, not to say painful, weeks ensured. Then curiosity getting the better of determination, I got all the mirrors in the house assembled in front of my mother's wardrobe. I examined my back and shoulders carefully. Almost there and then, I fell on my knees to render the Almighty thanks for mercy. The hump was going down. A baggy place in the back of my jacket could almost be seen, that was but lately occupied by the hump.

My career as a sailor at least would be secure again. Breathing deep sighs of relief I dressed, got out the green hat and went to strut proudly up and down the Botanic Gardens.

CHAPTER III

Mudlarks

We in our family were by no means the only people in Ulster who liked to have a view while seated on the throne of contentment. That was I soon to find out.

I learnt also that Bursie had valued my being under him, and the way I ran the daily errands without mixing everything up. One morning a message arrived notifying him that I was to be transferred to the reclaimer farthest out to sea, as a permanent cabin-boy. Bursie was furious, and stamped about demanding how the blinding this and blinding that he would manage now. But my fate was signed and sealed, and off I went, chugging down the miles of the great sea-lough. As I tried to keep my feet on the deck of a slippery mud-barge, my spirits flew up in joy to meet the gulls and terns that wheeled behind us.

Ungracefully, we sloshed over dreary, colourless waters between the sandbanks, until in a lop-sided sort of way we approached a large ship, moored some distance off the shore. A long pipe connected it with the sloblands like an umbilical cord. The ship's function was hardly romantic—it sucked up mud brought by the barges from the dredgers, and then pumped it through the long ant-eater snout to the shore, gradually building up the lost swamp land. Except for flocks of marsh birds and waders that flapped in great clouds at dawn and sunset, the reclaimed land was flat and deserted.

All around it lay country of peerless beauty, the woods and hills of Down. And across the other side of the Lough, lay the mysterious blue shores of Antrim. The waves in this part of the channel ran in with larger crests than farther up, and made more noise. Or perhaps it only sounded louder, because the titanic pulse and fever of the shipyard was miles away. I could hear the rasping of corncrakes and the anxious piping of redshanks, as the barge drew alongside. I felt that being on this ship would be almost like living in Fermanagh again, with the added thrill of being at sea.

The Bursar clambered aboard with me, and we went in search of the Cook, who would be my new boss. And there we found him, a little, thin man, gazing over the waves. He was seated on the lavatory, and the door was open. I could only think of our yard at home.

'Hey Cookie, on the nest?' said the Bursar by way of greeting. Then, without apologizing or moving on, he just stood there and introduced me.

Except for the nest, I was never again to see Cookie seated during the day. He was a fantastic worker, immensely proud of his surgically-clean galley. He sprang like a cat on any intruders he found stoking his beloved range to light spills for their pipes. No Ladies' Guild ever kept a church altar so lovingly as Cookie tended that old grate with black-lead and polish.

In the beginning, Cookie terrified me, despite his tiny stature. My principal work consisted of waiting on the crew at table. The messroom was below deck, under the galley. An almost vertical, smooth steel stair went down to the messroom from the hatchway in Cookie's galley. Through the hatch he passed me the food to take down below. Whoever, I used to wonder, had thought up such a system? This companion-way was the narrowest and steepest imaginable. It had absolutely no mercy on your spine should you slip and slide on your bottom from step to step. This could happen with alarming speed, until the lower deck was hit with a jolt and a clang. That I would ever descend it carrying a large tray, loaded with brimming soup-plates, seemed inconceivable.

Like a tortoise putting its head out of its shell, Cookie would lean through the hatch to watch my progress. This, of course, only increased the existing hazard. Safely arrived at the bottom, I would glance up and see the strong wind blowing his short brindle hair, that was as soft and pappus as thistledown. Should the tray hold six plates, I could reckon on a threat of ten bob being docked from my wages if I dropped them. But confidence soon grew, for I discovered that most of Cookie's terrible threats were uttered in a theatrical way, as much to relieve his own feelings as to terrify me. But he came to accept me, though this did not preclude much shouting and following of my progress down the companion-way.

Food being Cookie's sole means of expressing his higher self, it was natural he should be as temperamental towards his art as any artist. Most of his shouting bouts and tantrums resulted from war-shortages. He became terribly cast down if Bursie or the new message-boy failed to bring what he wanted to feed the fifteen resident men of various nationalities, besides other casuals from the smaller craft. What artist would not be angry if, seized with an idea, he found all his tubes of paint squeezed empty and none to replace them? Often, when Cookie had little food at his disposal or nothing much could be done with what there was, the men grew discontented. I would find Cookie looking through the hatch as I came up, to see the state of the empty plates.

Though Cookie's demands were meticulous, they at least had sound ideas behind them which he usually explained. But the men's fads over food were more difficult to remember, for I could see no rhyme or reason in them. There were those who liked lots of gravy. As I struggled on the companion-way against strong winds, Cookie's stare and the slippery steps, they would call after me, 'Give us a good wallop of the brown'. Their mates who could not bear to have everything awash in the rich dark gravy would make demands for a 'dry deck'.

During meal-times relations between mess and galley always tended to be strained. The crew was ever ready to defend its rights against an infringing cook or cabin-boy. The bull-juice caused most friction. Bottled milk never came aboard. Instead tins of sweet condensed milk were set on the table. Cookie meant it to go in the tea. But the milk went into puddings in great lumps, or it was laid over a slice of bread like mortar on a brick, or it was spooned straight into hungry mouths. And of course, none was left for tea. I would then be sent up to Cook with the empty tin and a pseudo-complaint about Cookie's tight-fisted way with milk.

A faint attempt to organize matters ensued to see that every man-jack got a fair dose of the bull-juice. Lucky Pat set himself up as a sort of mess-prefect. An uncanny run of successes at the football pools had earned him the nickname. This was almost a sufficient reason for prestige among the rest, without recourse to the authority of his greater age. Lucky Pat proposed to guard the tin of condensed milk which I got from Cookie before each meal. But the way of all flesh, or nearly all, is sweetness. Even Lucky Pat could not resist the delicious white glue. Neither could I. Guilt stole on him unawares sometimes, however, then he would consider it his duty to roar his disapproval. Unfortunately, the attempt to raise

Cain, had no effect whatsoever. His face was the wrong sort for being cross. He had a dropped eyelid and generally the contented look of a hibernating mole. If Lucky Pat should find no milk for his own tea he would seize the tin, cast his fully-open eye round the table and demand, 'Which white-livered-son-of-a-bitch left his muck scoopulatin' this here out?'

The tin would then be held up for a general inspection, and often indeed, there would be dirty marks from a careless, thieving finger. But the artful among the crew could deftly turn Lucky Pat's main issue aside. They tripped him up on his use of long words, most of which he invented himself on the spur of the moment.

'Scoopulatin'?' a scornful voice would question, 'ain't no such word.' In the furious argument that followed, during which Lucky Pat coined a dozen new words, the devoured tin of bull-juice would be forgotten.

The background to this sort of argument might be the incessant noise of the great pipes eating up grey ooze and sending it landwards. Sometimes too, the paint-chippers would be working overtime, their hammers beating without rhythm against the old boat's sides. Yet above all the mechanical din, Lucky Pat's voice would rise, assuring us by the Holy Boy that ere the sun went down the whole pack of us would be eunuchs if the next tin of bull-juice disappeared so quickly. But of course, it always did.

When the day's last meal finished, and the galley was shining and scoured, I breathed more easily. By evening, the morning seemed as far away as if looked at through the wrong end of a telescope. Each day was like a battle that must be won before nightfall. And somehow Cookie and I always emerged triumphant. But there could be no victory celebrations, for already warnings of the next attack rumbled on our

horizon—breakfast. Kippers and eggs there must be if disaster was to be avoided. Of all the meals, breakfast must go
well because the crew's morning work depended on it. But
what nervous exhaustion could result from the obtaining of
those kippers and eggs. When Cookie got up at five o'clock,
perhaps not so much as a slice of bread could be found in his
galley. Cookie anxiously looked over the rail, scanning the
first tug to come down, trying to see if the wretched message-
boy was on it with the precious supplies.

The younger men who had been in the Royal Navy behaved the worst on these occasions. They used the spiciest,
most effective language which could even make Cookie
wince. They were the men invariably late for breakfast, even
when it appeared punctually on the table. Cook had to begin
all over again then, for they would not be put off with leav-
ings. If anything went wrong, they demanded Cookie's
presence, and reminded him how much solid hard-earned
cash they paid for their food. Contemptuously one of the men
would hold up a brown egg that had sprouted knobs of con-
gealed white in the process of boiling. It never seemed to
strike them how lucky they were to get the eggs at all. After
being in the message-boy's case, which perhaps was searched
at the dock gates by the police, and then during the sea-borne
journey being slid around the deck of slippery barges, finally
to be hauled up to our reclaimer by a line—after all these
hazards it was a wonder the eggs arrived whole at all. And
once the crew nearly went on strike, because Cookie had produced such a tasty dish from a hare. They declared it would
make any children they might beget have hare-lips.

Even when Cookie exerted himself specially to please the
men, he would get a contrary reaction from some. The plates
always went down below piping hot, and tea or soup arrived
in the messroom only just off the boil. Cookie was well aware

how obnoxious half-cold food could be. Yet some country boys from the Free State would ungratefully ask, 'Will ya go and hang it on a bush?' My remedy was to remove the near-boiling liquid, put cold water in and then serve it again. Cookie would have died to know that his wonderful soup was diluted. Although it was their biting that caused their barking, like most grumblers, the latter was worse than the former. When they went off for a night in town, they never forgot to bring Cookie back a bottle of stout.

Washing-up after breakfast was child's play. I was soon down in the mess again. The crew not only ate there, but most lived there also. Consequently, its own peculiar odour pervaded the place, a compound of kippers, sweaty socks, and wet oilskins. It never occurred to me to stop and think whether I liked this smell. It was simply one aspect of the mess, which liking or disliking could not alter. Round the table were tiers of bunks, for the mess was the ship's largest cabin. Since daylight could not light it, electricity did. By its aid I swept the floor and tidied the bunks, always keeping a weather-eye open for the 'brown nippers', for Cookie had a horror of fleas. Next I got a bucket of water and filled the mahogany basin in Skip's cabin. This was used only at midday by a director of the firm. In all weathers, rough or smooth he appeared on board, wearing ? white riding mac, that made a stiff, important rustling sound as he walked.

No matter how many men might be calling for dinner in the mess, I had to leave everything, fetch a cloth for the tray and nervously carry the director's dinner in to Skip's cabin. He never spoke. Except once. He looked at me in disgust. Was it, he asked, an absolutely indispensable feature of my duties to plaster the food all over myself? Blushing like a beetroot I got out. A glance in the mirror solved the problem, for I could see nothing on my clothes. My hair-dressing that morning had been rather hurried, and there, stuck in my parting, was a lump of margarine, caught like a burr on a woollen stocking. Fastidiously, the director never failed to use the folding washing-cupboard. But the dirty water in the bucket underneath was so clean that I felt sure he only ran the tap just to keep *me* running about. I used to think that his mornings could not have been busy, or his hands would have been dirty. He seldom finished his lunch, which was some consolation to me for there was sure to be a titbit to wolf before handing the tray back through the hatch.

Chief's cabin lay next to Skip's, and on Friday I went into this also. For an ordinary member of the crew to see inside the chief engineer's cabin was a rare privilege. Although he ate with the men, Chief never let anyone into his living quarters, and he kept the door locked. Perhaps he thought somebody would play practical jokes on him because he was English. On Friday mornings, however, the key was mine, because I went in to scrub the cabin, being rewarded later by a handsome tip. His wife and children smiled photographically round the walls. Undoubtedly his wife would have smiled less broadly could she really have looked in and seen what a state the cabin got into by Friday. Hundreds of cigarette butts littered the place like fat, white maggots. They stared from the galley's tea-cups and saucers. Cookie always accused me of having broken these, as by Friday the crockery had been missing for a week.

I learnt to be quick over the cleaning below. With care, I could work in a free half-hour for myself before the dinner vegetables needed peeling. Quick as a wheeling gull, I was into a rowing-boat and pulling away from the ship towards the reclaimed coast. I did not go to the nearest point of the shore, for the cox and his mate had built a wooden hut there to live in so that they could be near their work. I headed the little boat towards the desolate plain of sorrel and bachelor's buttons. I had business to do behind a bush. Only once had I used Cookie's 'nest'.

In Fermanagh, before my confirmation, I had been given a 'private' talk, and this solemn, quite unhelpful affair, had included a warning about the effects of venereal disease. It was considered a great horror, not only because of its being God's revenge on sinners. V.D. posters were displayed everywhere during the war, so that even babes and sucklings could hardly avoid noticing them. Though we joked lightly about most sexual matters, 'V.D.' had a stark, terrifying sound. Long before puberty I knew that V.D. could make you go blind, or mad, or both, or kill you. I also thought that the innocent were in danger too and could pick it up from lavatory seats. Determined not to spoil my chances in life, I never sat, but always crouched with my feet on the seat! But only on one occasion did I perform this curious, hypochondriac act on Cookie's 'nest', for he discovered it, and practically threw me overboard.

On return from the waste lands, a stack of mugs would be waiting for washing-up. The crew loved tea at any time of day or night. It would not have been an exaggeration to say that Belfast harbour would never have been dredged but for all the tea that flowed into it. Not wanting to show their true feelings, the men called Cookie's tea 'bog water', although it was, in fact, as black as the awful molasses the great-aunts used to force down my throat. During this mid-morning break, enquiries were already going forth as to what might be cooking for dinner. Excellent a cook though he was, Cookie often found it difficult to produce interesting food, either because of the lack of meat or its poor quality. Undoubtedly, the big dough balls he served at dinner represented his *chef-d'oeuvre*. Whether they floated like icebergs in 'the brown', or were eaten surreptitiously with the forbidden bull-juice, we all loved them. It had to be admitted that, gastronomically, the 'bellyweights' went down like cannon balls.

After midday dinner and washing-up, a rest on deck seemed well earned. It was a rest only in the sense that no running up and down or climbing companion-ways took place. Though I was far from idle, with the sewing on my knee. The crew went through an enormous amount of clothing, and appealed to me to remedy the damage. This I did by means of huge patches tacked on to the largest holes. Unlike their reaction in other domestic matters aboard, when they were hyper-critical, the men accepted my tailoring services humbly and gratefully. A year before, I had found the sewing-machine at Maggie's farm irresistible, and could not rest until I made myself a pair of trousers. I considered this superior work to putting patches on dungarees. There seemed to be no end of ways for my talents to exercise themselves, for I also did the laundry and earned a lot of money.

Nothing, however, proved to be such an important apprenticeship as the barbering. Heads differ from trousers in that holes in the latter can be patched. The truth of this stood plain for all to see after my very first attempt at barbering. The effect was definitely of a moth-eaten animal in a taxi-dermists. I regarded my handiwork with not a little horror, for I knew the bald patches could not be concealed. By good fortune my victim was most patient and forbearing. Sus-picion born as my scissors plunged too recklessly into his hair, became fact when he looked in the mirror. 'God strewth,' one member of the crew was overheard to say to another. Poor Phil got up from the chair and said mildly that, 'Well, an' he would just wear his cap now till his head healed.'

Phil seemed destined for the butt-end of fate's blows, yet nothing could disturb his tranquil nature, not even my scissors. I never saw anyone so emaciated until I went East years after. When the wind blew off the sea and billowed inside his collarless shirt, I used to think it would carry him away. Once, when I lay snoring through part of the afternoon, Phil came to look for his clean linen. I woke to see his drumstick legs by my bunk. 'Beggin' yer pardon,' he whispered meekly, 'but I'll have me drawers, an' be gettin' away to town.' Not even Cookie would refuse the gentle but pathetic figure of Phil drying his clothes in front of the galley grate—a great mark of respect when even the Almighty Himself would not have been allowed in without Cookie's permission.

Before it seemed time, almost as though it played the day's last joke, the sun leaned heavily to one side of the sky. Nobody could stop its weight now from falling behind the far headlands. At summer's height, the conduits stopped gurgling and shaking the ship, and the paint-chippers ceased their hammering, while the sun still clung tenaciously like a bat to the blue roof of the world's cave. But later, as summer drifted out like a tide that would not return for twelve more months, knocking-off time and sunset drew closer together. Perhaps of any hour of the day I loved that most, when the first suggestion of night stole over the water. The buttress basalts of Antrim went first, melting deliciously before your eyes, dissolving into a region of indeterminate indigo. Then as the first night-winds scooped wave runnels along the ship's sides, you looked across for the woods of Down, and found them gone too.

Then from the grey mud-flats, a shimmer of sounds rippled over the Lough. The waders made the last protest of all against the thief who had stolen the sun. By straining my eyes I could see the restless movement that turned the mud into an aviary matching the mosaic of cries. The colourless seascapes and reclaimed sloblands reverberated with the birds' clamour, that seemed to be without individual voices, except for occasional strident notes or shrill laughter.

Disturbance of the idyll might come from Cookie's furious raking of the galley fire, though oddly, the metallic sound was not out of harmony with the waders' noise. Prosaically, a bucket of kitchen waste might plop into the water, to be seized on by ever-hungry gulls. A hardly audible sound on board, but none the less significant for that, was the flipping of cards. If the cabin grew too hot the men came up on deck. As they squatted or sat playing on boxes, the bowls of their pipes glowed red against the pale, fading green of the evening sky. Sometimes I would see the study of a face, well-known by daylight, in chiaroscuro. It would be a red monochrome, strangely softened by the faintest of lights from the pipe bowl.

In the bows, I had a favourite nook, hidden from Cookie's eye, and affording a view of the Lough mouth. Here the watery expanses stretched unbroken to the sea. On moonlight nights, the troughs between the waves caught the moon's light. Or sometimes huge masses of cloud would drift over. White sails seemed to be unfurled against the moon, the rounded forms passing like ships blown safely to distant sky-harbours. On some nights, as far as the eye could see, the whole sky was filled with processions of these armadas, crossing the wide sky-bay in squadrons. And under them, in real water came real ships. A royal ermine of foam trimmed their bows, and behind them a wake that rocked our reclaimer. These boats, low in the water, could be seen best by day. They had earned their ermine, for many had run the gauntlet of mine and U-boat. Fascinated, I watched them glide peacefully up the channel. How proud I was of those ships, and what sad thoughts possessed me as they came down channel on their way out. Then, their holds emptier, they went high out of the water, leaving only ripples behind. Sometimes I could see their propellers turning slowly, playing in the water like porpoises. But the high seas awaited them, and some, I knew, would not come beautifully back to Belfast, or any other harbour, ever again.

Passenger ships and those crammed with troops, were livelier than the cargo-boats, for plenty of people always lined the rails and waved as they went by. Occasionally they shouted things, especially soldiers who were bored with the journey and glad to be in sight of landing. Most disparaging remarks about our reclaimer sometimes came across. I always listened carefully to hear if there were any caged dogs aboard, yapping unhappily at their plight. Did anyone care for them if they got sea-sick?

Below me bobbed the nun-buoy where gulls perpetually fought to stand king-of-the-castle on its narrow top. Above me fluttered the strings of washing. With only these two for company, I sat in the bows softly playing my mouth-organ. The sad songs of Irish emigrants appealed to me, especially those my father had sung. And there were others learnt while I lived in the West, about young soldiers dying in the 'land of the stranger'. The melancholy wail from my mouth-organ often brought Griffith into the bows, with his accordion. Griff could really sing—the strange haunting songs of his native Wales, and in his native Welsh tongue too. Even when he spoke, music flowed in his voice, a lilting sound if he was happy, but plainsong when he had solemn things to say. Not even at country *ceilis* had I met anyone with such a fund of songs, or anyone so expert on the accordion. Griff's big, horny hands looked incapable of getting any music out of the yellow keys. Yet they played good accompaniment to his light baritone singing. Out of forgotten centuries, Griff conjured songs, all pure melody. Not so remote seemed the sound of harps long since gone to dust.

Each minute of the summer fell like a grain in a hour-glass that promised never to run out. A changing pattern marked it, of sun or rain, warm breezes redolent from the Down woods, or salty, unexpected gales from a furious running sea beyond the Lough mouth. Smoked haddock might replace kippers for a day, and the 'brown' might be usurped by a white sauce over salt beef. Seldom now did I pause before shinning up the vertical companion-way with my pile of plates. And although Cookie still bellowed, it lacked conviction, for he well knew shouting no longer scared me. I obtained a measure of independence. The firm provided me with a bicycle. Now in emergencies, such as the message-boy's non-appearance, I could pedal to the nearest suburb and shop there. And all day, every day, come wind, come weather, the pumps sent mud to the shore. The shore line was changing noticeably.

During my afternoon lull, Taddy's cheeky-cheerful face would grin at me over the side, as he climbed aboard. He never stayed long, but long enough to intrude on the routine. He was always full of news about men on the tugs and dredgers, though nothing took precedence over his latest ambition in physical culture. The sun had tanned him like polished teak. Energy flowed out of him; he could not keep still. Our afternoons invariably ended with horse-play. Taddy delighted in his powerful body and the control he had over it. Sweating and laughing we threshed about, safe because Cookie was not in his galley above us. Although he was older and better built than I, Taddy did not always have his own way for I could counter his stronger muscles with my longer reach.

The thumping as our bodies struck the deck, or as we

shouted at each other, usually reached a pitch that the outside world could no longer ignore. Lucky Pat would come down then, and roar at us like Doom.

'Quit the codology, an' git back to yer places,' he advised us, adding an encouragement, 'before I take the knife to ya.'

Doom indeed nearly did overtake us one afternoon. Taddy poked his head in the messroom door as I was ironing Lucky Pat's Sunday shirt. Taddy started wrestling straightaway. My protests only excited him. Lucky Pat did not come in until a neat, ginger iron-print had burnt itself indelibly on to his Sunday linen.

Perfect white shirts for Sunday Mass were necessary accoutrement for Catholics. Their blue serge suits made the shirts seem doubly white as they climbed into the boat. In such get-up they quite put to shame the rest of us, slovenly Protestants that we were, who would probably put on nothing specially to honour Sunday. And here we were—as many Mickeys as Billy Boys, at the entrance of the greatest Protestant city in the world, with never a word of religious controversy between us! From the deck I could look out at the Lough to where, beyond it, the Cave Hill rose up. Terror and mystery these caves held for me as a child. I used to imagine their floors and the bones littering them—the pathetic remains of Protestant children kidnapped by the Fenians. Obviously enough, I had never dared to go near the caves. My two years, however, in Fermanagh had put all such nonsense from my head. I had worked alongside Catholics in the meadows, had even slept in the same room, and discovered for myself how absurd our ideas were about their faith. So deeply affected was I by this new attitude, I had no intention of going back to my former Lodge of the secret Orange Order. On the reclaimer I had been moved to see a young

Free Stater, who had been particularly kind to me, cross himself before getting into his bunk. Nobody on our ship wanted anyone's blood, because, three centuries before, King Billy beat James the Fleeing at Boyne Water.

Only old Charlie saw fit to openly uphold the glory of William III's victory, and then he did it when drunk, simply to bait his rival, Lucky Pat. Perhaps because he lived alone on his barge, Old Charlie came in the outsize range of characters. Occasionally he came to eat on our ship. He might have allowed himself exaggerated mannerisms to assert his age—which was certainly greater than anybody's in our crew. But few were nimbler than he, and none would have risked his neck at the open mud-hole of the barge, as did Charlie. With a gammy leg, he hopped around the hole's narrow rim, ignoring the wild swerves his uncertain legs made now and again. He would have drowned in the ooze, had he slipped in. Some spirit must have protected him. Indeed, he looked not unlike a monk, for his head was bald, except where a pure white tonsure circled it above his ears. His fleshy, ashen face seemed beyond the reach of circulating blood. Its surface had been so deeply pock-marked, that it looked as though hewn out of pumice-stone. And his eyebrows appeared to be simply the ends cut from the length of hairy twine that held his trousers up. In spite of his prepossessing, shaggy appearance, Charlie could not abide being called 'Father Christmas'.

Although Charlie rigged himself out in comic clothes, and walked in a funny way, there was unmistakable dignity and command in him. You don't handle a huge barge all on your own, without being something of a skipper. He could throw a rope, at precisely the right moment, so that it never missed its objective. Currents ran in the channel, which could sweep the barge away if the ropes missed. Never once did Charlie falter. This never ceased to amaze me for the old man suffered from a trembling, as though he stood perpetually in a bitter wind.

The trembling caused our great friendship, for Charlie could not shave himself. He did not invite everyone to his cabin, so to be asked was an honour. It belied the mucky cargo and perpetual slime that covered the rest of his barge. Below deck, he had the finest accommodation in the whole of Belfast harbour. The interior had been completely renovated and displayed a fine nautical style, with pitch-pine boarding and beautiful oil lamps made of brass and opalescent glass. They were seated in swivels and rocked gently as the barge rocked, casting soft night beams round the cosy room.

Their kind light fell principally on the faded photographs pinned to the walls, discovering amid palms and velvet the plump forms of donkey-fringed girls. Charlie claimed to have known and loved them all. The charms that lured him were hardly shown to advantage by the straight, shapeless dresses of the 'twenties. At least, Charlie said he knew them in the 'twenties. I was no expert in those days, but nevertheless a suspicion haunted me that the buxom ones had blossomed before the Great War. Amongst the non-white girls were one or two frightened-looking negresses for whom old Charlie had a special partiality. His 'black dollies', he called them affectionately.

Like an anchored boat slewing into the current, the old bargee's conversation inevitably turned to the topic of his former loves. If he had a few drinks inside him, the photographs would come down from the walls to be embraced and kissed. On a shelf he even had a plaster model. It was of a woman standing with a greyhound, painted grotesquely green and gold. Charlie hugged this also when beer fanned the dying flame in him. That such thoughts could linger behind his rather startling face, surprised me the first time I saw

him drool over the pictures. But I supposed it far better than
that he should mumble to himself. Charlie never sounded
bitter that the days and nights of real love-making were over
for him. Of course, he assured me, with a glitter in his eye, if
the war had not been on, he would have been off like a shot
to the dolly-dives of Cardiff. South Wales ports, apparently,
were thick with brothels, and could even provide a dolly-
mixture of colour and race. 'I'd be there,' Charlie said. But I
doubted if he would.

A lawyer's skill was needed to deflect old Charlie from his
main topic, and get him on to the really interesting parts of
his life. Once the girls were out of mind he could re-create
most fantastic situations. Getting the girls out of his mind,
however, was the difficult part. Charlie had roved over the
whole globe. In the process he had involved himself in everything a sailor could, from knife-fights in doss-houses to his
part in the famous grain-races to Australia. Such stuff was
chicken-feed compared with his diving for treasure—real
gold! Even in 1917 it had been valued at five million pounds.
And this was not the gold that Captain Kidd looted from
Peruvian churches, and buried on the shores of Great Sal-
vagen. Although the British Admiralty hunted that pirate's
hoard, they were much more concerned in old Charlie's
affair. Thousands of gold bars lay on the ocean bed, off the
rugged Donegal coast. The Admiralty knew the exact spot,
for it marked the grave of nearly four hundred men who were
the crew of the *Laurentic*. A floating mine struck the great
ship, and she went down. Charlie rushed to the scene as one
of the first divers.

As Charlie told me this tale for the tenth time, the barge
cabin vanished and instead I saw heaving seas and huge waves
smashing the treacherous coast. I heard the hurtling winds,
and felt the rolling decks as the lead-booted divers sank into

the sea. My heart contracted with tension as the ghostly, frog-like forms sank on to the huge submerged hulk. Not only did it lean at an impossible, dangerous angle on the seabed, but it rested in a minefield. Mines were always exploding. The divers never knew in the enfolding water, whether the explosions came from above or below them, for they had to use explosives themselves to blow open the liner's steel carcase. But worse than these perils was the water pressure. The *Laurentic* had sunk twenty fathoms, and the awful pressure at those depths made the divers bleed internally. The battle went on for years, and in the end most of the drowned millions were salvaged. Gold, apparently, suffered less of a sea-change underwater, than on the Exchange.

Rather sadly, Charlie would hold up a trembling hand, and twist the ring on his finger. I thought it rather a large affair for a man to wear, until I knew what it represented. Charlie felt more pride in that ring than in any other possession. It was his souvenir from the diving, a sovereign, part of the bonus given for his services. He had blown the rest on dollies years ago. But not the sovereign-ring. It was better than a V.C.

Old Charlie amazed me during one evening session, by introducing a topic other than girls, himself. Would I, he asked shyly, like some 'portree'? I imagined this to be an offer of bourtree wine, for which I had a great liking. Anticipating something good I said, 'Thanks'. Charlie fumbled about in a drawer and pulled a piece of paper out. His own scrawlings covered it. The 'portree' turned out to be his own bawdy poetry in praise of the dollies, yellow, black and white. Obscure both in form and content, Charlie's 'portree' sounded even more so because he had no teeth. To get any overall view of his theme also proved impossible. Charlie stopped at the end of every line to explain its subtleties, thereby confusing an issue by no means clear from the start. All the same, not without a dram of truth, I told him that such 'portree' could not be matched, even by the best.

Charlie's toothless gums impeded things on a more material plane than his verse, notably the shaving. Unlike my new-discovered hair-cutting, I was an old hand at wielding a cut-throat. At the age of ten, I had regularly shaved a drunken, bed-ridden musician, so I knew all about it. But the sight of the naked steel blade put all thoughts of dollies and 'portree' from Charlie's mind. He sat, tensed up with nerves, on the chair, breathing stentoriously through his mouth. He had to inspire in this way, because I was holding his nose. I used thumb and forefinger, a method I considered proper to my task. Neck, jowl, and chin were easily negotiated, my firm razor strokes felling the bristles as surely as a scythe in a hay-field. But when I came to the area immediately surrounding his mouth, the ground, so to speak, would collapse beneath me. Poor Charlie sucked his mouth inwards, and the more I urged him to relax, the greater became the suction. Fear of severing the upper from the lower part of his face, prevented me from exploring the cave with the cut-throat, and consequently, Charlie always wore a hoar-frost circle of whiskers round his toothless mouth.

When the shaving operation was completed, the old man would jump up and examine himself in the mirror. If pleased he danced a little reel to himself, lame leg and all. Indeed Charlie was very fond of jigging, and when he and Lucky Pat had their biggest quarrels, Charlie always danced.

His wildest moments occurred, naturally enough, on Saturday nights. Like every other civilized creature not on duty, Charlie went into Belfast, returning at an hour when old men ought to have been in bed. Except for the scratching of my pen, no noise disturbed the cabin on that particular

Saturday. My thoughts flew far from the Lough, across to the West and Maggie's farm. So many questions I asked her about the high summer on the fields I had loved. Deep inside me, I felt indignant that a letter had to be written about such things. I should have had the right just to walk out the door and see for myself, just as I had at the last harvest. If I went through the cabin door now, I should smell no sweet meadows, and the night air heavy-scented from honeysuckle in the lane.

However, a sound from the outside world penetrated my lonely dream. I held the pen in mid-air, certain that I had heard a human cry, like somebody falling overboard. I strained, listening, my own blood singing in my ears. But I could hear only the channel silence again. The incoming tide ran round the ship in uncanny gurglings, and ferreted desolately through the sloblands. Otherwise there was nothing. I began to write again. Then, unmistakably across the water came Charlie's fusillade of abuse. I guessed immediately what had happened. Our ship's ferry tied up by a wooden wall of piles holding back part of the new land. Two alternative ladders could be climbed to reach the little boat. One of these was damaged. The waves leapt up at its bottom rungs, then fell away with horrible regurgitations, amongst the limpet-scaly piles and seaweed tresses. Charlie had come to the slimy green wall, and started down the ladder with the missing rungs. His parcels had gone into the water and were swallowed.

I got him safely to the ship, but nothing would induce him to get away to the barge and bed. Most of the other men were already in their bunks, trying to smoke themselves to sleep. But Charlie's whole Saturday shopping was gone. What annoyed him more than the loss itself, was the galling thought that the money might have provided more porter. And he could blame nobody but himself, nobody had been pushing or hurrying him when the parcels splashed, into the Lough. He complained at such length, repeating the exact details, that Lucky Pat told him pointedly to shut up—'Can't ya cessify?' Charlie was pleased now that his vexation had penetrated the consciousness of a fellow being. As some attention is better than none, and as sympathy was not forthcoming, Charlie decided to make the best of a bad job, and play Lucky Pat up. It would relieve his feelings, if nothing else. Lucky Pat then told him not to be such a 'blinkin' eegit', which was all the old shellback needed. He gave an Orange toast with every mouthful of porter, good, old-fashioned pledges like:

'Here's to the glorious, pious and immortal memory of the great and good King William who saved us from slavery and knavery, witchery and bitchery, thuggery and buggery, brass farthings and wooden shoes, and to hell with the Bishop of Rome. And he who will not drink this toast may be crammed, jammed and rammed down the big gun of Athlone, and may I be there with a flaming flambeau to touch him off, and may he fly round the world like bees round a treacle pot on a summer's afternoon.'

Nobody took any notice, not even the young Free Stater who crossed himself and wore a Sacred Heart badge. After one or two more inflammatory pledges, the porter seized control and old Charlie became sentimental. Parcels forgotten he began to sing *The Wearing of the Green*, which brought Lucky Pat from his bunk to share the evening's remaining drink. Before the night was out they were both quite tight. Like a couple of naughty children they went off to forage in the galley. Who cared about either King Billy or the Pope, when there might be a couple of cold sausages on the go?

I had odd twinges of home-sickness for the farm and occa-

sional dreams about it. But the feeling that I belonged to
County Fermanagh and not Belfast Lough, did not cause
much disturbance in my otherwise happy hours on the reclaimer. To me this life was a splendour of pitching decks, and
chugging, oily machinery, of hectic hours in the galley's
steam and in the smelly mess. And there were cycle rides
across the eerie reclaimed moor. Often I struggled against
salty winds on a last errand to get supplies for the next morning's breakfast. Each day held unique excitements. Strange
objects embalmed in the barges' mud—a piece of a human
body, tortured metal from a shipwreck—might be found by
the men, and they would call me to come and see the wonder.
And in the evenings a rich variety of amusements were at
hand if not on our own ship, then aboard old Charlie's barge,
or on some other ship to write letters for the illiterate, and
once in a while perhaps a party.

So the days passed.

Then the fitful gusts of summer turned into days of gale
and nights of down-pouring. The sun that on some days had
melted pitch caulking now hardly appeared at all, and in-
differently when it did. Living conditions down below changed
to a dank, dismal affair. Wet oilskins and dripping sou'-
westers were never out of the way. The men's bright spirits
lost lustre, moodly silences became more frequent, and
Saturday night booze-ups more violent. Yet it was not this
that disturbed me.

I had been writing often to Maggie and Christy. All my
anxious questions brought heart-breaking replies. Maggie, of
course, did not realize the effect they would have on me, she
merely tried to slake my thirst for news of the farm. The hay
by the spring-well was rotting in the swathe. The rabbits had
not left so much as a blade of corn in the Fort field. The
clamped turf was as wet as dung, and Maggie could neither

get to, nor from the well without losing her one plimsoll and one wellington in the mud.

Only a few months had passed since I left Fermanagh. Now they seemed yawning, empty eternity. I dwelt on the previous summer as I clutched the companion-way rail. By that time we had already made the last sheaf into the harvest-maid to be hung indoors as a blessing on the next season's crops. But the blessing had surely turned into a curse, and all the crops rotted in the fields, and all the calves I had helped into the world were destined for sale at the next fair.

Without realizing, I began to watch for the post's arrival. No matter how Cookie might shout about burning saucepans, I tore open the letters from Fermanagh. And one morning came the news which precipitated events. Maggie wrote that a large nail had gone through Christy's foot. With country obstinacy, that made people determined to walk to their own funerals, Christy was hobbling about with a stick. I knew, also, that he would first try cures from all the local charmers, before consulting a doctor.

I half-blamed myself for this accident, as I had just sent Christy a big tin of orange paint for the hayshed. He got the injury while painting. This played on my mind, and the letter burned in my pocket against my chest. A few mornings after, when the men had gone off to work and I sat alone dissecting my breakfast kipper, I was overcome. I could not bear to think of little Maggie having to wheel the milk churns down the long, humpy lane, to catch the early creamery lorry. She and her brother had given me security—their whitewashed Fermanagh farmhouse amongst the soughing elms was really home.

My fork dropped with a clatter on the plate. I resolved to run away, back to the West.

CHAPTER IV

On the Run

For a whole year, after being evacuated from Belfast, I had planned to run away, back to the city, to its fish and chips and twice-nightly cinema. A great number of evacuees did, in fact, go back. But each time I got my case filled, and was ready for a dawn or midnight flight from the misery of early bed and boiled potatoes, the billeting officer appeared. And most of the new houses he found for me, scattered among the lakes of the West, had something to commend them for at least a few weeks. Inevitably a crisis arose and I prepared another escape. When Maggie and Christy took me to their hearth and made me their white-headed cub, I never wanted to leave.

I would never have thought that one day I would be a fugitive from my own family. The Island, and a 'trade at my back' were things I had accepted all my life as an irrevocable fate. Yet here I was, revoking it, the very shipyard that my mother had won for me patiently over the years, as a favour from Black Tom. Big 'Ina knew that the proper apprentice-ship could not begin until I reached sixteen, but she insisted that I must have 'my cards in the firm'.

Looking back into a bitter perspective, my mother could see the ranks of our family and, among them, so many un-

employed labourers with no skills. Some of them at best had
been no more than humble rope-makers. Belfast might boast
the world's largest rope-works, but Big 'Ina could only recall
with the bleakest feelings her early years in the works. The
back of her neck was very brown, like a gipsy's, and she often
used to say as we washed her back on Saturday night, that the
rope-making had caused it as a girl. Not only had her own
life been hard, but so had those of aunts, uncles, and cousins
who knew no trade. My mother determined a higher fate for
me. For as long as I could remember, my entry into the shipyard was her sole aim. That done, she could rest. The morning I left the house in my new dungarees to meet Black Tom
at the Island gate, she had winked her eye, and laughed light-
heartedly. The great dream of her life had come true. My
'cards were in' and there they would stay.

Well, I supposed, my cards would stay, even if I did not.
My breakfast kipper grew cold and was finally scraped un-
eaten into the waste bucket. Maggie's letter was in my shirt
pocket, a single sheet of paper driving a great wedge between
my two lives. Yet as I tidied the mess cabin, I knew perfectly
well which side would win. Accordingly, I packed my things
into my case. During the afternoon break I slipped over to
Charlie's barge and was taken up to the noisy harbour.

Now my heart began to thump against my ribs, echoing
riveters' hammering in the hulls. Nobody would question my
suitcase, because I always took one for the shopping. They
could not know what lay inside. Under the gantries, over the
wet cobbles, past the black-clothed workmen, past the fore-
men's sheds and drawing offices. And so to the gates, the stitch
in my side threatening to cripple me, my shirt wringing with
nervous sweat. Surely the policeman at the gate would see the
state I was in, stop to question me, and open the case. But he
only nodded as usual, and I went through.

On the Run

The docks' long goods train impeded the way. I could not wait for it to start, or to walk round it, so I scrambled under the mushroom-like buffers between two wagons. Half-running, not noticing the busy afternoon streets, I came to the Great Northern station. The day's quickest train to the West had gone. The next did not leave for hours. Relaxing a little, I felt the need for food. Although some danger remained that somebody I knew might see me, the worst part of my escape was over. Until that day I had never eaten in any place swankier than tea-and-bun transport cafés, or the long wooden hut in Enniskillen where the farmers went on fair days. But there seemed to be such warmth and glamour in the city's smart restaurants. Gleams of light from shaded lamps on wet afternoons, the glint of silver on tables, always looked so rich and tempting. I decided to find one, and celebrate the joy of going back to Maggie and Christy again.

Complete with case, I ascended the carpeted staircase to a café over a very select cinema. Gentle illumination, the murmur of discreet voices, the tinkle of superior spoons in superior cups, rose out of the room, like ozone from the sea. Because it was full I had to share a table with a young man and woman. Their voices, at least, were not discreet. Perhaps they were theatricals, for they spoke in a gay, euphonic way, and occasionally others nearby would turn to stare when they laughed. Cigarette smoke coiled round them like Art Nouveau foliage.

A slim, supercilious waitress, cuffed like a nurse, glided across and supposed that nobody had taken my order. I said no, they hadn't, and that I wanted pie and peas please. Her pencil, on the end of a chain like a nun's rosary, tapped with slight annoyance on the order pad. 'We're only doing teas.'

Everybody in the café seemed so happy and well-fed. Their clothes were smart and none of them seemed to have any work to do. How different from the grease-ingrained, sweat-smelling men of the shipyard. And everyone had a companion to talk with, except me. I kept my eye on the swing doors. I would already be missed on board. A slight pang assailed me as I thought of Cookie getting in a panic about the men's tea, with no one to help him. Would they think I had fallen into a mud cargo, or been injured in the shipyard? Several alarming ideas occurred now, that I had not thought of before. Evidently my escape was not quite so simple as an evacuee running away home. Doubtless the police would be notified. Though they would not think of looking for me in such a café, I began to count the minutes left before the train went and I would be safe in the West. The curly gilt hands of the restaurant clock seemed hardly to move at all.

A diversion from my preoccupation appeared in the form of a middle-aged army officer with church organ-stops for eyes, who carried a ridiculous little cane. He looked about him, and made for our table. Did he use the cane for beating his soldiers, I wondered? He looked the type. Was it made that length specially, so that he could conceal it up his sleeve, and then flash it out suddenly on the poor soldiers' bottoms? I took out Maggie's letter. But I only pretended to read, because I knew it off by heart. Now that the army man sat so near, I became aware how different the young couple were. The officer smelt, not so much of polish and Brasso as of *polishing*, of khaki colour rather than cloth and leather. Yet the young man on the other side of me gave off a smell of perfume, quite distinct from that used by his girl-friend. Perhaps it was only the warm air bringing out his hair-dressing. The girl glanced at me now and again, and I wondered if my margarine on top, newly applied that morning, was exuding too.

I felt relieved to see the officer wince when the couple gave another stage-laugh. The girl had kicked a shoe off under the table, and the young man was hiding it. It seemed odd for two smart grown-ups to play like that in a swanky restaurant.

'Where in hell has she gone?' said Major Bull's Eyes to me in reference to the waitress. It eased his embarrassment over the couple, to start blustering about something. Folding it carefully along the original creases, I put Maggie's scruffy little note away. The officer made me nervous. A sergeant-major in the Irish Guards who had once taken Big 'Ina to a dance was about the highest I had ever spoken to before. And this be-crowned man would insist on addressing me about the 'perfectly foul' weather, and the bad service in the restaurant. I was secretly pleased that the waitress treated him in the same off-handed way as she had me. It tickled the young couple's humour no end when the waitress tartly reminded Bull's Eyes that 'There's a war on, you know.'

He cornered me at last. Something conversational had to be said.

'What's good for rickets?' I asked him.

The organ-stops were pulled out for a good crescendo.

'I *beg* your pardon?'

His fingers abruptly stopped their drumming on the table, and I realized that even the theatricals had cut short their giggling to listen. Maggie had ended her note with news of my pup which she feared had got rickets. I thought this such an intelligent subject for a grand tea-party with a major! He made a sort of grunt, and said not another word to me. Instead he stared at the window, though he could not see out because it was steamy.

When the tea left in the bottom of my cup had got a streaky sort of film on top, and the teapot had gone quite cold, I considered it time to leave. The woman at the cash desk charged an enormous sum, it seemed enough for a whole day's meals.

It was worth it though I thought, with the carpet and velvet curtains and everything. I turned round at the door, and saw that the theatrical couple had taken Bull's Eyes into their confidence. They stared at me lugging my case awkwardly through the glass door. I was glad to get down the stairs and into the city crowds. The going-home, rush-hour had already begun.

My fear that someone would see me vanished when I arrived at the station. Hordes of soldiers thronged it, adding ochre to a grey background. When the train for Londonderry came in, a rush of soldiers, loaded impossibly with kitbags and rifles, surged along the platform. They blocked the doors like bees going into a hive. The clatter of their boots filled the whole train, their kit blocked passageways and weighed down the luggage-racks. Although their compartments had not been reserved, the men resented any attempts at civilian intrusion. Eventually I was allowed to squeeze my slender hams between some friendly Scots. But I suspected the invitation was because of my suitcase, which they set across their knees and began to play cards on.

Belfast soon faded. No regrets possessed me as the train pulled us away from the city, shabby with war-neglect, drab with September rain. Though firmly wedged in by the soldiers' thighs I had seen our own house trembling by the sidings. Our old tom-cat was crouching on the yard wall, like a furry snail. An early design of mine for an arch of the Orange Order on the gable of the return room had almost disappeared now. With a bit of slate I had scratched it graffito-wise in the cement rendering. But years of exposure had dulled its once-sharp lines. Our gable had never been painted the elaborate way that many others had. All we could boast was a magnificent Star of David, executed in sumptuous gilt. I had stolen the little tin of paint from Smithfield Market. Its

bubbly-gum smell so intrigued me that, after finishing the
star, I used up the remainder by painting gold rings on each
of my fingers too. That was something to show-off with at
school. The teacher failed to appreciate my adornment and
tried to flail the rings from my hands with her cane. Only the
slightest trace remained now of David's Star.

After leaving our house behind, and the rows of houses
straggling out to the Bog Meadows, the train picked up speed.
The very lines under us had led me West two years before.
How I had changed since then! Singing and whistling
through towns that would soon be incognito under the black-
out, we leapt through cuttings, and exploded into dripping
tunnels, rushed through gloomy woods, snorted by quiet
pastures where the humps of cows could be seen as ink
patches in charcoal fields. But when we came to Omagh,
such splendid pace-making came to an end. Fermanagh-
bound we had to cross the bridge and board a local train. It
was decidedly a country-bumpkin of a train, and almost had
straw sticking out of its funnel instead of steam. I was still
with the Scots and we all made jokes about getting out to
push. The train jolted us as though going across ploughed
fields and not rails. We came to Fintona Junction and swore
that the comical horse-drawn tram, waiting to take people
into the town, was faster than our own train. At every wayside halt, we seemed to stop for hours, letting out great gasps
of steam. But at last Bundoran Junction came and went, and
we crossed into Fermanagh, the most beautiful county in all
Ireland, I was sure.

Only one more stop occurred before the end of my journey
at Enniskillen. This penultimate stop was Ballinamallard. I
leaned out of the window to see if the little porter would
recognize me. Nearly two years had passed since I fell in the
river here while out poaching one night. Afterwards I had

to be dried in the little waiting-room with the mail-bags.

A balm fell on me as I handed my ticket to the man, and stepped into a darkened Enniskillen. My last time at that station had been miserable enough. The clinging straws of doubt, as to whether I had done right to run away from Belfast, were whisked away by reed-scented airs blowing off the lakes. What a fool, to deceive myself into thinking the shipyard life was a good one. I made no pause at the station but hurried through the streets, as fast as the suitcase would allow me. A heavy lorry overtook me, full of soldiers from the train. Its great tyres swished on the road, and for long afterwards I could hear its engine grinding away in the distance. I hurried up the church bray, seeing only chinks of light that an air-raid warden would soon obliterate. Aloof from the eyeless houses, the cathedral clock gave alms from its chest of solemn seconds.

As I crossed the far bridge, to get off Enniskillen's island, a black figure emerged from the lake mists. I discerned a gun in his hands. The police-guard demanded my identity card. Setting the case on the ground, I fumbled in an inner pocket. Surely they had not caught up with me already. Had the people in the smart restaurant phoned the police? But the guard only grunted as he looked at the grubby card. Fortunately it still had the farm address on it. The case intrigued him but he would not open it for examination until we got off the bridge. Did he really think I had a bomb in it? Satisfied, he vanished as noiselessly as he had come.

Six miles lay before me now. But the walking did not matter. I was going home. Nevertheless my case, which seemed light enough at the station, grew heavier with every step. And the restaurant's thin slices of toast had done nothing to reinforce me for such a walk. I hoped that Maggie had not given the remains of supper's stirabout to the dogs.

On the Run

A moody moon slid between the clouds, and silver blushes raced across the fields. Unlike the town streets which were dead when deserted, the lonely countryside teemed with movement. Hidden by hedges, secreted by woods, a million missions by night animals went on all around me. I kept alert, hoping to see the glint of a badger's eye, or the dainty, wary trot of a vixen down the bogpass. Could those soft thuds be the quicksilver dive of weasel through a turf-clamp? Leaves rustled loudly in a moist, warm wind that would bring more rain soon. Little streams ran by the road, or dodged through culverts, pretending under cover of darkness to be mountain torrents. Owls swooped and guinea-fowl piped simple, sudden notes from wayside roosts, as though disturbed by dreams. The McGurtys owned the flock that lived in a tree overhanging the road, two bog-banks away from the house, but nobody ever interfered with them.

I realized how hot the miles of case-lugging were making me. But I dismissed the idea of resting. All I wanted was a sight of Maggie's lane. Already I was coming to home-ground. Here stood the schoolhouse amongst the blackcurrant bushes. Its windows seemed to wink at the ex-pupil, as he hurried by in the fitful light, his hands heavy but his heart light. I was never frightened to be alone at night in ghostly lanes, or to follow the road through dungeon-dark woods, knitted branch to branch overhead. But it was a relief, never-theless, to hear human voices, when the first gate-house of the mansion-house appeared. In spite of the late summer's terrible weather, they at least had got their turf won, and such a stack of it piled up, as to dwarf the privy. Each place I passed now had associations with people I knew. Wasn't it the talk for weeks when one of the neighbours had gone mad and dashed into the lodge demanding, 'Butter and eggs, me neck's bust! Butter and eggs, me neck's bust.' Before they came to take

77

him away, he had devoured quite a mountain of dairy produce.

Changing my case from hand to hand, I came to pools of shadow on the road cast by trees whose twisting limbs were as familiar as the lines in my own palm. And I knew the names of dogs which rattled their chains in the moon-washed stillness. Through the box-hedges I could see cottage chimneys thurifying the night with their simple frankincense of turf. This perpetual offering ceased neither by day nor night, summer nor winter through generation after generation, for ill luck would visit the household whose fire went out.

So far I had not passed or seen anybody. But at the head of the tiny chain of lakes that we called 'our own', I caught sight of Biddy O'Brien. She came out for turf, no doubt to rake her fire. I thought it sad that she should hop so badly from infirmity. From the road, you could see she was getting the outer wet turf to bury in the white ashes. By morning, they would be red embers that she could boil her kettle on. Holding up her pinny, she filled it with turf, making her silhouette absurdly pregnant—and she over eighty, and with almost no hair! Biddy held an intimate place in our regard. She had a very fine well, properly constructed in stone. As a young woman she used to bale the water out in an annual spring-clean. Stark naked, she climbed down into the empty well to scrape its fine walls clean of all the mosses and slime. Maggie's father once came upon this strange well-nymph. But although this happened nearly seventy years before, nobody could forget it because the story was handed on. I thought it poignant, for now Biddy could barely hop as far as the steading to lock up her hens.

Lit by the moon's uncertain taper, the road twisted on, becoming more familiar with every yard. I had to go up a little bray before getting to our lane. An old orchard ran along one side of it. Nobody used it, except the cubs on their way home from school in the autumn. The gate leading into the rows of tangled unkept trees was a noted spooky place by night. Grass grew up and covered the gate's lowest bars. The joints, so carefully made by a carpenter of long ago, had dropped and opened. Curious wood lichens grew along it. A family of fungi had occupied its rotten posts for years, with fleshy flanges like cake-stands in a baker's window. Haunting the orchard gate was the ghost of a little girl in white confirmation clothes. She only came when death lurked in our neighbourhood. I had so often longed to see her. But, of course, I had never got 'the gift'.

Our lane ran off a minor road that tinkers loved for its camping sites. Lush green verges for tethering caravans and horses, stretched for most of the way beside the unmade-up track. When I turned into this road, I kept my eyes open for signs of the tinkers' latest camps. You could always tell, for though romantic, tinkers were always such untidy people, leaving empty food tins about. And they let their fires die on the ground like gutted David Stars, making no attempt to cover them afterwards. And not only did they plunder the henhouses and take rabbits out of traps, but Robbie Jannings said that they were so grand that they would not use God's own moss when squatting, but Robbie's cabbage leaves.

Tendrils of dog-rose climbing to the hedge-top seemed to lean out towards me like fishing rods with a heavy catch. For the first time since coming out from Enniskillen, I stopped properly. A vast peacefulness rested over the shadowed forms of trees and hills I knew so well. I seemed to belong so much, it was hard to believe I had ever gone off in the spring-cart with Christy, back to Belfast.

Half-way up the lane, I hid my suitcase in the pine plantation. It would still be too early for the farm boys and girls to have finished their *ceili* up at the house. My homecoming must be a private, simple affair, shared only between Maggie, Christy and me. If everyone saw me arrive, none would leave until every drop of news about the big city wonders they had never seen, and my life there in the past months, had been pumped out of me. Another night, perhaps, I could stand it, but not tonight. On leaving, most of the people would cut across the hill on foot, following sheep-runs or Maggie's little track through the rushes to the spring-well.

Those with greater distances would have come on bicycles. Without a sound I walked up to the house. Nothing, it seemed, had changed. The squares of windows where the *ceili* was in full swing glowed with friendly yellow light. But those of the parlour and hall were mere black holes in the whitewashed wall. When the moonlight came flooding across, the panes of glass glinted. I could see every unevenness on the walls then, and the metal geometry of a bicycle leaning against it.

I recognized it at once. The big basket on the front gave the dilapidated old machine away. How many times had I seen the bag, dropping as though with dropsy on to the front wheel, when crammed full? People round about thought this accessory a great affectation, for only the 'quality' had such baskets. Indeed, this was undoubtedly the reason why Ivy Melfern had the basket fitted. Nothing could be too smart for her. For one thing, young and old alike must address her as Miss Ivy—no plain Ivy's, thank you. Not that, beyond her personage, Ivy's life contained any grandiose elements. God had given her a robust frame, heavy enough to match its height, and He had filled it with vigour. She housekept for two aged, distant cousins down the road. Though superior, Ivy did not despise labour with her own two, more-than-adequate hands. She cut turf as well as any man, and could follow the plough.

A strange love-hate had existed between us. Perhaps for months not a word would pass, though we might see each other in the bog regularly. Then came the sport of the spring turf-cutting, and we would roll each other in the heather. For unknown reasons, hate always prevailed over love. We never parted except on the worst of terms. I used to think that this was because she acted so grandly—and her only coming from people who had but the grass for three cows, and an egg basket seldom heavy enough to pay the travelling grocer! Admittedly, Ivy had a dozen or so ducks of her own, that kept her in dresses and Sunday collection. The cousins' brother had risen to be sergeant in the police before he died, leaving the four hundred pounds which, rumour said, had been put away as Ivy's dowry. Because of this, she was not without her following.

Everyone who came to make a *ceili* at Maggie's and Christy's, simply walked in the back door, even Mr. Robert from the mansion-house, who took his tea 'in his hand' like the rest of us. But not Miss Ivy. Oh no. She would pound on the big front door knocker like the angel Gabriel himself, and have all the locks and bolts and chains undone for her. These foibles could be forgiven. But what I never could forgive, was the way she called Freddy their farmhand 'our serving boy'. Although both had been 'saved', and both frequented the same preaching-house, Freddy and she were not often on speaking terms.

Both also slept in the loft of the small, thatched farmhouse. Naturally, Ivy occupied the best room, the one over the kitchen because it was warmest. Like Maggie's, and most other homes around, this room was not enclosed, for the stairs went up into it, and it acted as a big landing, giving access to the smaller rooms. Freddy consequently had to pass Ivy's bed to get into his own little loft. The cause of Ivy's complaint was that, on some mornings, Freddy stole so quietly into her landing-bedroom that she did not even have time to pull the sheet over her head. Had Freddy seen her stark naked, she would hardly have felt her maidenly modesty more outraged. Miss Ivy's first question, on being admitted through the front door's bars and bolts, was to know if 'our serving-boy' had also come to *ceili*. If Freddy had, then Ivy would be shown up to the freezing parlour.

I pinched the tyres of Ivy's bicycle to see how hard they were. I would certainly not go into the house until she came out and lit her spluttering carbon lamp. Excitement at coming home decided me against frightening Ivy. In spite of being 'saved' she believed in ghosts. Manytimes I had jumped out at her from the old orchard gate, as she pedalled dreamily by. Instead, I collected some apples, and went to sit in the hayshed. One by one, I heard the visitors coming out. As the back door opened, a gust of voices or laughter blew out, and the calls of 'Goodnight and safe-home'. Was this how lonely tinkers felt, always on the outside, when they spent a night in somebody's shed?

Midnight was not far off when I heard Maggie. Her voice gave me a thrill. I longed to push out of the shed. But she was escorting Ivy down the lane. Why couldn't they hurry? Twenty minutes must have slipped by before I heard Maggie come up the lane again. Time now had to be allowed for Maggie to go into the garden for her late-night office. When I thought the moment ripe for my surprise arrival, I tiptoed across the cobbles and peered through the kitchen window.

I saw Maggie washing the vessels after the evening *ceili*. She sang one of her milking-songs as the crockery chinked together in the tin bowl. Besides herself, nobody was there

except Christy. He was sitting with his back next to the hob.
I pressed my nose against the glass so that Maggie could see
me. But although the table where she washed-up stood right
by the window, she saw nothing. Perhaps her glasses were so
covered with flour from the morning baking, or maybe the
wire-netting at the window obscured my face. The wire had
been fixed inside to stop the hens from going through the
glass. Such a panic seized them after sneaking into the kitchen,
when anybody went in.

Then I was in, laughter mingling with tears that were not
all caused by the shallots which Maggie promptly cut up for
the wanderer's supper.

As if to give a good omen, the moon shone out full and
clear, unshaded by clouds, when I went into my little white
room off the kitchen. The moonbeams showed me nothing
had been altered. Maggie could not hide her pleasure and
excitement, and to honour my return, she brought me the
big parlour lamp to undress by. My day had been long and
exhausting, and I soon doused the lamp. But under the moon,
my little room hardly dimmed. Stretching out in the soft bed,
I waited for a never-failing night ritual—Christy loading his
rifle against intruders. Its click was the symbol of security,
bodily and spiritual, I found under their roof.

By the time the cuckoo had jumped out of his brown nest
on top of the dresser, and cuck-ed the single hour of one, I
had burrowed deeper into the great feather tick, and fallen
fast asleep.

CHAPTER V

Men Only

Maggie suspected nothing until the grocer's van stood at the end of our lane on Tuesday. The two young vanmen were late. They honked the horn irritably. This was to make us hurry down with the buckets of eggs which Maggie sold every week. But Maggie could not, or would not, just drop her work. She had to put on a clean apron and put her false teeth in to greet them. And this in spite of the fact that the two lads often came to *ceili* when Maggie seldom wore her teeth. Still, the Tuesday grocer's call was a ritual and rituals could not be disregarded. Besides, who knew that as she stood at the lane's end the vet or the rector might not dash by in their cars.

News and fascinating gossip about distant neighbours also travelled with the van. Naturally its scandal value was not so great as that of the Catholic Friday lorry full of papish fish. Maggie could only use this in emergencies, for to give our Protestant trade to the 'other side' would have been a disgrace.

After the important discovery that Mrs. Montgomery's pullets had started laying and that Charlie Price's stirk had fetched £14 at Derrygonnelly fair, we settled down to business. Our eggs had to be weighed, for in those primitive pre-peace times, they sold by weight. The efforts of Maggie's hens consequently determined, for instance, the number of loaves she would buy. Shop bread still belonged to the realm of luxury—visitors had it served in preference to home-made bread as a delicacy. Shop butter from the creamery also held a social position higher than home-churned butter. Visitors ate it on their bought bread and considered themselves honoured. This was nothing but a conceit, for the home-made things tasted far better.

Along with these refinements of living, Maggie laid in her stock of oil and candles. During the war even light had to be fought for occasionally. Sometimes the battle with grocers was lost, and we had to sit by the leaping flickers of the open fire. Maggie told the vanmen that I had come home again and that she would want a lot more provisions, the same amount in fact as she had taken before I left for Belfast. In her innocence, Maggie forgot that this required another ration book. When the vanman asked her for mine she blushed guiltily. Of course I hadn't got one. Poor Maggie began to make all sorts of excuses, but promised to give them one next week.

This unforseen snag upset the careful concealment of my escape. I too had overlooked the ration book problem. Even here in the depths of the country, far from the belching war chimneys of Belfast, body and soul could not be held together without red-tape. I knew at once there could be no way out but to write to my mother, tell her the whole story, and ask her to collect and send my ration book. As I led the ass-cart back and forth from the hayshed with rucks salvaged from the fields, I felt uneasy. At any time I expected a policeman to appear in the lane on his way to arrest me. Big 'Ina was not the one to stand nonsense.

By the vanmen's call on the following Tuesday, however, not only had the law not materialized, but neither had my ration book. My mother had not replied. This seemed ominous. The situation at Maggie's now became difficult for me to handle. In order to screen her from alarm at my desertion I had informed Maggie airily that, at completion of the dredger work, the firm had given me a sort of holiday of unspecified length. The non-appearance of the ration book, however, proved hard to explain away. Before a month was out a letter from Belfast did come. The handwriting could be mistaken for no other, for my sister always penned Big 'Ina's letters. Anger seemed to invest even the crossing of *t*'s and the dotting of *i*'s. I was certainly having no ration book forwarded—only orders to get home and ready to start work again on Monday morning.

A single molecule of me, but no more, felt slightly relieved at this order. I had not bargained on the complications that would result from my return to the West. I had helped Maggie and Christy to save quite a bit of the hay. But I would hate to involve them in trouble. It would be too terrible if they should have to go to court and perhaps even have their names in the newspaper, for harbouring the runaway. The nervous tension of awaiting discovery, each day's uncertainty, had rubbed quite a lot of gilt from my gingerbread. At least it would be good to have a clear conscience again. Not only had I deceived my mother, but Maggie and Christy also.

Perhaps a deeper reason existed as to why I did not altogether resent going back to Belfast yet again, a reason I may not have perceived at the time. It was simple. Far from being severed for ever from Fermanagh on leaving it, all I had to do was walk on to the train in Belfast, and several hours later there I was, back again at Maggie's. Having done this once, I could do it again, and whenever I wanted to. When I was a child being evacuated the journey had seemed interminable, so that on parting from Maggie's to go home to the shipyard, I imagined we would be at opposite ends of the world. Now I knew otherwise.

Though sorry to lose me again, Maggie accepted the demands of work as inevitable, especially as she thought me to be only on holiday. I struck a bargain with Big 'Ina. I would go home again provided she did not make me go back to the shipyard. The ignominy of returning to the reclaimer and being laughed at by all my mates for running away could not have been borne. This problem, however, solved itself. My mother had been to the firm to collect my 'cards'. They gave her a full pay packet which had accumulated, because the firm thought I had been ill. But they no longer kept the job open for me. Land-reclaiming could not be held up because of an absentee cabin-boy.

Poor Big 'Ina, she must have thought bitterly on my ingratitude as she took the 'cards' out of the place which to her, signified security for me. Finding a job by myself was not without allurement. Who could tell into what fortune or adventure I might fall? Meanwhile the newspaper advertisements must be thoroughly combed in the 'smart young lad wanted' columns. To assist my application, Maggie cycled all the way into Enniskillen, and bought me a marvellous book about letter-writing including instructions on how to address archdeacons and viscountesses.

Of course no job turned up by the specified Monday. The atmosphere that developed in our house at Belfast rapidly deteriorated, as I restlessly moped about. Harry was anxious for me, on Big 'Ina's behalf, and failed to see why I could not get work. Often we resorted to fists, and very noisy fights developed. One victory was secured—the choosing of my own jobs until I reached sixteen and could be properly apprenticed to engineering.

Every day I answered many advertisements. Such flocks of doves flew out of my ark, but alas, few returned again. Most of the employers stipulated that applicants must write in their own handwriting. I guessed that my tiny, cramped cursive could be blamed. But at last I was asked to a warehouse for an interview. Three or four other boys also turned up. An old man dealt with us. The glasses through which he peered at us had a temporary bridge of red sealing-wax. He was taking no chances on our ability, and set us a test. The interview allowed him to vent a latent desire to be a schoolmaster. Marshalling sheets of paper, he set us to discover the cost of so many rolls of something priced absurdly in farthings per foot. Whether or not my reckoning was correct, I could not tell, but the job went to the smartest young lad amongst us. Perhaps the complexion of flawless pink enamel, and the impressive array of pens and pencils in his breast pocket, did the trick. He looked so fresh and healthy compared with the rest, and somehow *clean*, whereas we had spotty, blackheaded faces. I also showed the first sproutings of a beard, that clung like swan's down indefinably round my jaw.

Another dash to get the evening paper followed this debacle, another mad rush to get the dozen replies into the 'box-number' department in the city. It became plain after several days that my pathetic notes were getting me nowhere. So I limited my selection to jobs where only a personal interview was required. This policy immediately produced results from a gents' outfitters. I walked in, stated my case, and got the job. No serious competition faced me, however, because the wage offered could hardly be called a wage at all. It was not even a third of what the shipyard gave me. But I was quite prepared to stand the loss, for was I not being up-graded from mere message-boy to training assistant in the underwear department?

No delay between appointment and commencing work could be allowed. The shop was busy and short-handed. I must begin promptly next morning. Before the little manager put his various keys in the shop's various locks, they expected me to be standing outside. Without me apparently, the whole thing would get off to a rickety start. As soon as the door was opened, I had to run up numerous dark flights of stairs and put a large kettle of water on a slow gas. The time it took to boil had been carefully observed through the years, and was reckoned long enough for me to go downstairs and sweep right through the sale-rooms. Then up again to find, amazingly, the kettle singing. It had then to be poured in a bucket, to which I added a bottle-cap full of pine disinfectant. The minutes now were counted before Madam should arrive. She both owned and bossed the shop, a woman of great girth and vast punctiliousness. With my mop and bucket I had to take the stairs as fast as could be, and have all the dog dirt washed from the front windows before the boss made her grand entry. It would have surprised you to see what proclivity the Belfast dogs had for the apricot boarding along our windows.

With my mop left hanging out of the window to dry, like a mediaeval head on a pikestaff, I descended once more, prepared for the great world of outfitting. Although at the beck and call of all and sundry, I was supposed to be learning the ins and outs of the underwear stock. There was none of your X- or Y-fronted brevity, but good ankle-length drawers and sound Christian combinations. Such things of course never saw the light of day, but were kept in a strictly moral fashion in a room at the back, discreetly lit by an electric lamp. A lot apparently had to be learnt about such garments. Before the shop would allow me to become a proper counter-assistant, I had to know my stuff. Not so easily would they let me loose in the sale-room. I was longing to put the customer's money in one of the round wooden boxes. You pulled a sort of lavatory plug that sent it across the room on wires like a mountain railway, to the cashier's glass office.

The underwear, I discovered, had special ways of being folded, each item demanding a different method. And all were wrapped in cream paper. Far more complicated for me than the knots and bows in the wrapping paper, in which the firm specialized, was the esoteric pricing system, a peculiarity of the trade. Not only had I to inscribe this strange sign-language on each parcel, but on pieces of card the size of postage stamps, equipped with sharp wire tusks. These then had to be fixed to each garment, every handkerchief, every pair of braces. Thus converted from nonentities into particular identifiable beings, if not with a name, at least with a number, the clothes were then stacked on wide shelves on the wall behind. Even here the piling took place in order of precedence and size.

On asking, of course, no customer could realize what his enquiry for a woollen vest might entail. Six parcels would perhaps be undone to find exactly the size and quality desired. Imperiously, the counter-assistant would push the parcels aside when he had rifled them. It was I who had to tie them all up again. And should two or less pairs remain, then I had to climb up to the stock-room to complete the half dozen.

Old men who came in, sometimes young ones too, rarely knew their sizes. So while they stood looking foolish at the assistant's inquisition, I went round the counter. I nearly garrotted them in endeavouring to peer down their necks and tell the tell-tale number on the back of a vest. Pants were more difficult and often meant fighting through an extraordinary barricade of belts and braces, pullovers and shirts. So often the assistant would purse his lips and announce, 'Yes, I thought about a thirty-eight. I've a lovely job in interlock. Sure you've got your coupons?' Few things made us more cross than undoing a mountain of parcels only to find the customers were couponless.

The shop people expected me to be like a Hindu god possessed of a dozen arms and legs, with which as many jobs could be done simultaneously. While measuring a shapeless waist Miss Till might call from the other side of the shop, 'Hop upstairs, Longlegs, and get me an outsize bib and brace in blue.' Our shop catered very much for the rougher workman's clothes as well as the real gents' Tootal ties and Jaeger half-lengths.

Miss Till was rather sweet, and I found her nickname for me not unattractive. In her mouth it sounded better than it had done in school years before, when I had been terribly thin for my height. Although still long and adolescent, my legs were beginning to fill out, and I knew that by the time I was fully grown they would be perfectly all right. So she could call me Longlegs if she liked, and I would take no offence. In fact I liked leaping up the four flights of stairs to put the kettle on for her lunch. Everyone took sandwiches for midday, and ate them in the attic in relays. Unfortunately Miss Till's time seldom coincided with mine. One day, however, I followed her up and she dropped a hair-clip on the stairs. I treasured this for weeks, until it led to a big row at home. One of the lodgers in my bedroom stood at the window watching the passing trains, when I walked in. He was staring absently across the lines. But in his hand was Miss Till's clip— being used to clean his ears out.

Madam herself never appeared in the lunch attic. Reliable sources reported that she went to the Grand Central Hotel.

But she could still manage the stairs, as indeed I discovered the day she went up and found I had choked the kitchen-sink with tea-leaves. I always swallowed my sandwiches quickly, as the room soon turned into a hen-party. Knitting needles clacked, while I got roped into holding skeins of khaki wool for the older dears making comforts for the soldier laddies. Indigestion tended to result from the thickness and solidity of my sandwiches (how frail Miss Till's were, so precisely gauged to fit her Cupid's rose-bud mouth) but nevertheless I bolted out for some fresh air as quickly as possible.

At that period of the war, a site just off Castle Junction had been conveniently cleared by the Germans. The space left by their bombs provided two men with an arena in which to perform wonders with their bodies. Clad only in a sort of bright bathing costume one of them reclined gracefully on a bed of nails, with an apparent minimum of discomfort. Meanwhile, the other balanced a ladder surrealistically on top of his head. At the end of the ladder, up in the air, a chair was balanced, its height to be measured only against the bomb-scarred, stranded fireplaces of the next building.

These delightful, but entirely pointless feats, were varied by a display with a sledge-hammer. The one who had lain on nails reclined again, but on the ground this time, while his mate gently laid a paving stone on his chest. I thought it must feel cold until I thought of the insulating value of the thick mat of hair that entirely covered, not only the front of his torso, but the back too. With pirate ear-rings rocking like pendulums, the man swung the sledge-hammer back over his head. He paused infinitesimally before bringing it down with an almighty crack on the paving slab, and of course, his mate underneath. The crowd's gasp of apprehension changed to one of surprise and approval when the hairy stooge leapt lithely to his feet, throwing off bits of stone like a surfacing mole. I could not help wondering if the Resurrection morning would be similarly spectacular.

While the sledge-hammer man was tearing a couple of thick telephone directories in half with his hands, my interest in the men suddenly vanished. An Inst schoolboy standing next to me said the whole thing was easy. The great volumes had been baked in an oven first, and were so brittle that they practically fell to pieces in the man's hands. I was as much flattered by a public schoolboy making-up to me, as I was astonished by the quackery.

Back in the shop, there was no time for regrets at the fickleness and fleeting glory of the stunt-men's world. For an hour I wrestled with an impossible mountain of vests and drawers, left from lunch-time sales. They lay strewed about in a tangle of limbs composed in a tortuous maze like a swirling ceiling-painting of the Last Judgement. When order had been brought to chaos and the intractable undergarments folded and stacked away again, another hectic hour ensued. This time it might be spent with the window-dresser. Here again my part was played back-stage rather than at the footlights, for my lot fell to undressing, rather than to dressing the windows. Because the German air force had given no guarantee that it would not return to raze yet more buildings, our windows were partly boarded up. All that remained was a square of glass in the middle, through which window-shoppers gazed like fish in an aquarium.

On demounting the display, I had to find the right home for all the caps and collars, scarves and socks, gloves and gaberdines, belts and braces. The dummies had to be stripped. And when the window-dresser began to reconstruct his empire, I picked out the large price labels, printed in an endless arithmetic progression, that advanced by sixpences. More complicated mathematical series intruded in a favourite

11½d. The dresser would call out 'Seventeen and six', growing quite cross if I did not produce the card immediately with the deftness of a conjuror.

Without doubt the most enthralling part of window-dressing was the magnet. Dozens of dropped pins littered the floor and they had to be jealously collected. Holding the red-painted horseshoe magnet close to the floor, I went along, as careful as mine-detectors I had seen in war films. The pins shot towards my hand like rain bouncing on the pavement. Fascinating minutes could be whiled away by trying to make the magnetized pins hang together in chains, or pick each other up. Unfortunately, the assistant did not share my thrill in such experiments.

Poles apart from this entertainment was the carrying of bodies up and down stairs. Some of our window-models were awkward old brutes and resented clean clothes. Those that came out of the attic concentration camp hated my washing and grooming of them. The fixed, toothy smiles took on a contemptuous leer as my soapy rag removed the dust from their bloated, beige faces. Not one of them looked really healthy in spite of being spruced up. You would have sworn that untimely death from thrombosis threatened even the bonniest. A few were snobs. One monstrous beast called Ernie positively hated being forced into a common boiler-suit after spending a week in a fine Donegal tweed overcoat.

An inmate named Sammy had to be taken down the road one morning, to our branch shop. What a performance he involved me in. His main objection to the transfer, of course, rested in his prudery. How terrible to be seen in the street wearing nothing but a brown paper smock! Sammy battled all the way. Considering the permanent state of rigor mortis from which he and his mates suffered, he did very well. Everyone in the street watched me as I went by. It could have

been no worse if Sammy had been shouting about Basil
Brooke at the top of his voice. And passers-by would try for
a glimpse of Sammy's anatomy when the wind blew open
his paper smock, as if he were a kilted Scot. He twisted and
turned, and had to be shifted from hip to arms and back
again. At one point while I was concentrating on the crowd
to see that he did not get his head or arm knocked off, his feet
went smack into the bosom of an on-coming dowager. In his
panic at the crowds, whom he normally saw only as an
audience, Sammy nearly put his feet through another shop
window. What ignominy, I thought on the way back. Never
again would I allow myself to be so degraded.

Compared to Saturdays, weekdays had the peace of the
cloister on them. And Saturday was late-closing too. On my
first one, I thought the whole male population of Belfast had
come into our shop, to revest itself in underclothing. My
fingers became quite sore with tying and untying so many
parcels. But the tide retreated eventually, leaving behind the
flotsam and jetsam of crumpled bills and tram tickets and
forgotten gloves. The last wooden box went sailing on its
wire across the ceiling, and thumped down the shute into the
wire tray. Next, I presented myself at the desk. Although I
had spidery legs, like Ronald Searle's thin roué in the Lemon
Hart advertisements, I felt tiny in front of the huge bronze
cash register. I stood there, not daring to murmur, until
Madam spied me from her secret corner. This sanctum was
never penetrated by us lesser breed. All we could get was a
glimpse of the electric fire, the knitting patterns, and Madam's
own teacups, up-turned to escape the dust from my floor
brushing.

I felt even smaller when Madam took command of the
register. She spread herself amply over the seat. Her fingers
poised over the keys as if entertaining Saturday-night crowds

on the mighty Wurlitzer in the cinema nearby. The tune she played to me, unfortunately, was worth no more than a ten-shilling note (the oldest and dirtiest it seemed) and two half-crowns. And even then, I had to wait for the cashier to come and denude my wages for the insurance stamp. I never found out how the other staff got paid, for of course I was never on intimate footing with such godlings as the male assistants. They were all 'Misters'—one even owned a car and had been to Blackpool.

None of us cared for the Saturday rush, and neither did Miss Till. Certainly not after the big row. Madam had only just left a trail of footmarks over my clean floor first thing on Monday morning, when the storm broke. Her fire in the sanctum had been switched on, and a brick of setting sun greeted her (the double-bar only went on when she sat down). Madam was in the act of taking a half-bottle of milk out of her bag, when in walked a man. Could he talk to an assistant who had served him on Saturday? Yes, probably, but which one? Well, he couldn't be sure she was in the shop just then. His voice sounded loud, its tone touchy. Madam sallied forth, possibly thinking he was obstreperous. When the man could not see the assistant in question, we rightly decided that he wanted Miss Till, now doing relief down at the branch shop. But before Madam would telephone for Miss Till to come an explanation was necessary.

With a rush the man unleashed his dammed-up emotion. Well, on Saturday he had come in for a hat. . . . Deviously he described how no hat had taken his fancy so he left the shop. On getting home he found that he had come away with a new hat while his old one was left behind on the counter, because of the Saturday rush. Madam boiled. The telephone wires down to the other shop became red hot, and Miss Till was ordered up as fast as legs would carry her. Meanwhile, the old hat was discovered in a box. Such dramatics took place that the man faced Madam squarely and said that if he had known what was going to happen, he would not have been so honest. He left. Madam went into her sanctum to cool down, and Miss Till into the lavatory to weep. It really tore your heart to hear such sorrow. Poor Miss Till.

I was far from happy myself, however. The shop had its moments I had to admit. But at that particular time home seemed to have none. My mother had started going to work again, though the lodgers stayed put. This meant that we had no properly organized meals. In the mornings we squabbled for slices of black toast. My lunch frequently consisted of no more than a couple of buns. And for supper I often ended up with fish and chips, bought and eaten on the way home. It was horrible sitting down to supper in our house, I thought, and not being served until after the lodgers. In my newly-emerging adolescent assertiveness, I could not bear the way Harry sprawled in front of the fire, smoking an innocent pipe. Nor could escape to the parlour be made, for my elder sister Cissy was closeted with her American boy-friend, and Big 'Ina had placed a strict ban on the room. Not that I minded Steve, the soldier, too much, for he gave me several pairs of silk socks. Home was a dead loss. Most evenings I drifted into the cinema, and afterwards went home and straight to bed, speaking to no one, and not even going into the kitchen.

Such strains could not last for long. The climax came when I went to the dentist. For nearly a week, excruciating pain in a back tooth had kept me awake at night. I poured bottlefuls of essence of cloves over it. But the pain grew worse, and when it could be borne no more, I looked for a dentist. I went on a Saturday night after our rush and late-closing. Officially the surgery had been closed for hours, but the little man who answered the door in his braces seemed to read misery in my eyes. He took one look and said, 'Ah! my goodness, yes,' and put me straightway into the cold, hygienic chair. While the lamps glared and the anaesthetic in my gum took effect, the dentist chatted. He was very friendly, and on learning that I was only fourteen, called his wife in to guess my age. The poor lady blushed and said she supposed nineteen or twenty. Their son had just gone into the army and I was certainly older-looking than he. This pleased my vanity no end, for I always told the girls I was seventeen— old enough to be taken seriously.

Cracking like a walnut, the terrible abscessed tooth came out, and handkerchief to mouth I went home. I bled quite a lot in the surgery, but the dentist assured me it would stop, and gave me a pill. In good faith I went to bed. Next morning I woke to find the pillow and bedclothes soaked in blood. It had penetrated the mattress, and fell like peony petals amongst the yellow roses on the linoleum. Despite being very weak I managed to get out of my shoulder-straightening wireless aerial, before being rushed to the Royal Victoria Hospital. Various doctors and attendants treated my mouth before the awful socket stopped bleeding, for apparently my gums were diseased. Later I was told that my father's had been also, and that he suffered from it all his life.

Sunday dragged by, and although on Monday I should not have done so, I went to work. After all there was no advantage in staying at home. Weak, and feeling thoroughly wretched, I prepared to start the cleaning. But the shop seemed like Augean stables that never would be cleaned. The manager found me and saw at once how ill I was. He looked rather frightened, possibly thinking also that if I collapsed on the premises there would be a shindy with Madam. So he packed me off home again.

An hour had passed, but darkness presided in the house.

Nobody had taken the black-out blind down. The night-shifters lay humped still asleep, and not a bed was empty. Unless any of them had a bit of porter in none would get up until the late forenoon. I was unwanted. Even reaching over for my clothes in the marble-topped washstand, brought protesting grunts from the two railway stokers. You could smell their young sweat on coming up the stairs. Despairingly I surveyed what should have been my own room, thinking bitterly that when I wanted to lie down, there was nowhere to do so. For all they cared I could die.

I went down to the kitchen and wrote my mother a note. As she worked on night-shift and was herself in bed, I could not wake her. The first one to get up would see the note on the mantelpiece and read it. Big 'Ina would know soon enough that I had gone to Fermanagh again. For instinct warned me that only on Maggie's farm could I have the quietness and fresh air and attention that would make me better. As Big 'Ina worked at night, and had so much on hand anyway, she would hardly miss me. In the note I promised that when well I would return to Belfast.

For once the fact that everybody read my letters served a purpose. All the lodgers would know I had gone and they might dissuade my mother from making a fuss. I folded the scrap of paper down the middle and stood it up. It could not be overlooked. How it annoyed me normally, this reading of other people's letters. At the farm, letters for me had always been handed to me intact or I could get them directly from the postman. Maggie and Christy would have died rather than look at my correspondence, without my consent. This had confirmed my independence as a man. But on coming back to Belfast, the people at home treated me as if I were still a child, and my mail was public property. What rows there had been when I came in from work and discovered that post for me had come during the day, but the letter had been opened and enjoyed by family and lodgers.

Quietly the front door closed, and I got to the station well in time for the day's best train to Enniskillen. The journey seemed negligible now. Hardly glancing from the window I slumped in a corner, just waiting till the island-town came into view. Walking the six miles between Enniskillen and Maggie's farm was out of the question. Apart from weakness, I did not want the bleeding to start again. A hire car would solve the problem. I reckoned an hour's ferreting on the hill when I was well again would repay the cost. In the under-taker's shop I sat amid the sombre reminders of the grave, awaiting his grand saloon. Maggie's sister-in-law always hired the car at Christmas for a shopping spree, so I knew what it looked like. I did not, however, expect the door to be opened for me, nor to be ushered into the spacious back seat, as though I were the bishop about to go on a progress along the country roads to confirmation. The man sat in front with his gloves on, and generally put all the grandeur at my disposal. But I did not dare rest my hand on the leather strap at the side, as the episcopal hand did, in case it put another bob on the bill. And of course the vast saloon had not been built for bumpy lanes like ours, so the man set me down by the milk-churn stand at the top.

Maggie saw me walking up, and hesitated for a moment, not quite sure who had come to see her. Then she was dashing down to meet me, insisting on carrying my case. 'Robbie,' she kept saying in a distressed way, 'you're so pasty looking,' and within minutes had me in bed. I sank into the grateful crisp-sheeted bed, realizing in the first moments of relaxation how awful the week-end had been. From my little room I could hear Maggie get the trivet down and stand it in the hot ashes, to make me a milk pudding. She stirred it with a favourite ash-rod that I had planed for her. Now and again she would whip it out of the pot to chase after the hens that wandered into the kitchen. Sweet sounds—I was entirely happy now and at peace. No tired shunters and dirty stokers were going to push me over, and no night-shifters wait irritably while I got up, so that they could get into my part of the bed. All belonged to me, the whole farm was laid at my feet like an offering. Already Christy flew on his bicycle into town to buy invalid foods and other stuff from the chemist's. The Aylesbury ducks tumbled in and out of the stone trough by my window, and the clatter of pheasants blew in from beyond the meadows and dying rose-garden.

I woke, feeling fresher, finding that darkness had smothered the steading noises. A candle had been set in my room, its flame spreading a soft twilight over my calm little world. Not moving, I lay and watched the golden flame go giddy with the window draught, or leaping up like a dragon's tongue, trying to catch the ceiling cobwebs that also moved in the draught with exotic whirls. Then came the easy, languid march of hob-nailed boots. The first one had arrived to *ceili*.

'Didn't yer cub come out of the town in quare style,' announced Cahir the old woodman, before Maggie could hush his voice to whispers. I grinned in the candlelight, thinking how everybody knew already that I had come back. Half sitting up, I called out to Cahir, for I wanted now to communicate with life beyond my door. Maggie's head peered round at once, her eyes full of solicitude. Did I want the door ajar? Sure a wee rasp on the fiddle would do me good, commented Cahir, and Maggie had to tighten her bow and wait for my order. And Cahir could not countenance my choice of *The Old Bog Road* without giving a bleat himself.

'Here's wee Maureen, she's dying to give you *Moonlight in Mayo*.'

So it went on, all through the evening. As each and all arrived they sang a song for me, or told me of the bargains at the last fair, or who had been caught smuggling goods across the border. And Cahir of course knew exactly which tree bark to get for my gums—hadn't it worked wonders for the Colonel's parlour-maid? On leaving they promised to come next night and see me. Christy saw the men out, and Maggie accompanied the females as far as the bog-hole.

By the time the fire was raked, and Christy loaded his rifle upstairs, my candle had spluttered and gone out in a volcanic crater of white cumulus wax. A great, deep silence rose up now from the hushed countryside. Only the donkey stamping on the stable cobbles disturbed it—my donkey though, and my silence. Surely it was not the *last* full moon that had shone in here, glistening on the counterpane, the night I escaped from the shipyard? Or was it the moon of a hundred years before? Time did not matter any more. So far as I was concerned, the lodgers at home could sleep on forever—the gents' outfitters could be given up to corrupting rust and moths—and even Miss Till could marry an American soldier and I would not worry.

By the end of the week, Christy thought, the blue heifer would calve, and in a fortnight the thresher could come!

CHAPTER VI

The House that Jack Built

Winds blowing fresh over the West hills had brought the flush of health to my face again, by the time the thresher arrived. During the day we were busy hedging the big Fort field, or mowing rushes and bracken as bedding for the byre and stable. The blue heifer now had full rights in the byre by presenting us with a fine bull calf. And although her tight little udder was difficult to catch, she proved to be gentle and a good milker. Two weeks accustomed her to the odd touch of human hands about her, and I could sit on my stool without a kick. After my first days of rest, strength seeped back into me, and at first light I was already up, as in the old days at the farm. At dusk too I was out round the traps, renewing familiar but forgotten contacts. Perhaps I did not remember how a fallen tree trunk lay, or how dawn light turned 'our' chain of lakes to pewter plates. Nothing had changed while I was in Belfast. Besides rabbits and foxes, I still found stray rats in my traps, and sometimes an unfortunate cat, a dog, bird, badger, weasel or woodcock. My savings were going up by leaps and bounds.

That year we had little enough to feed the thresher when it eventually came. Rabbits had wrought destruction without mercy in the fields. The panting machinery could not be kept going for long. Nevertheless, the thresher's advent was a great occasion, and all the neighbours turned out in the usual way to keep the work going with a swing. In our kitchen afterwards, we made the traditional sowens by soaking some of the grain husks for a week or more. When it had fermented into a kind of sharp tasting mass Maggie put it through a sieve, and let it boil until it thickened. Then it became a very weird porridge indeed, reckoned to be a marvellous blood-purifier. It certainly sent us hurrying down the garden in record time, if we over-indulged it.

In the afternoons Christy and I cycled down the road to old Mary Brown's, to turn her cow over. Mary was a curious old soul who lived alone. Her renown derived chiefly from the collection of telescopes which her father had got from the castle where he worked as gamekeeper. The first time I ever saw the brass-bound telescopes was one Sunday after Preaching. I had only just arrived in the district as an evacuee, trailing with me a bad reputation of forever changing billets. Old Mary gave me a piercing look and said, 'Sure, ye've the green eyes of a wanderer.'

Although the telescopes occupied me for the next hour, I could not dismiss Mary's comment about my eyes. I thought they were brown. Back at Maggie's I examined them in the mirror. Mary indeed observed correctly. The eyes in the mirror looked green all right, a soft emerald fringed with pale golden rims, like a strange liqueur mixed from the two kinds of Chartreuse. But the wanderer's eyes did not displease the old girl, and during our first encounter she insisted that Maggie and I go down to make a winter *ceili* with her. We loved to visit the tiny thatched cottage. Should Maggie and old Mary become too involved with local gossip, I could always thumb through The Diary. This shared fame with the telescopes, and as said by many to be worth 'a sight of money'.

The House that Jack Built

The Diary was no more than a record made by the old game-keeper of his journey to a married daughter in Scotland. It did not strike me as being such a powerful story. Most of it consisted of lists. The remarkable numbers of grouse shot on the Highland moors each day was shown with descriptions of food, and comparison of prices in Ulster and Scotland.

'Have ya got as far as the "great pansies"?' Mary would ask during a lull in their conversation. The sister had dwelt on a ducal estate and one day during the father's stay, the duchess drove up in her carriage. The old man's baby grand-daughter was in the pram. Her Grace thought the child had such beautiful eyes—'just like great pansies'!

Eyes altogether fascinated Mary. Nobody was allowed past her half-door if she disliked their eyes. When a neighbour was sent for trial for murder, Mary declared she had known it from the woman's eyes. Animals also, apparently, showed their character by their eyes—especially her Bess, the cow who was a fine lady, as anyone could tell by a glance at her placid velvet orbs—though to be sure, Bess was a brazen shop-lifter, and always invading our winter kale and Fraser's orchard.

Christy, too, found an interest in Mary Brown, though mostly because Bess worried him. Mary was very fond of the beast, which rather resembled herself. But it was a nuisance, for not having other cattle, she never knew when it was bulling. She usually called me in to conduct Bess on these abortive courtships. Before handing me a crumpled banknote for the fee, old Mary told me to make quite sure that a 'second jump' took place, just to 'play safe'—a habit which the farmer hated. But the cow's day was done. It had con-ceived, and lost its calf-bed, and had been hurt in a bad fall. The fall meant that poor Bess had to be manually turned over every day from one flank to the other. Four neighbours convened in the byre to perform this operation. But despite our efforts to make the animal comfortable, despite endless feasts of hag-tapers, bantam eggs and the finest gruels, the cow died. And it was not because she worried over what the city people might get in meat tins, that old Mary refused to let the bone-house lorry take the carcase. Instead we had to dig a fine grave for it, and near the house. Mary wanted to guard it from sacrilegious tinkers and prowling dogs.

The bad summer and rabbits between them had done their worst to Maggie's and Christy's crops. But I had done my best to lessen their effect, and once more had to think of Belfast. I smelt trouble in the air. Long silences from home always indicated this. Whatever happened Maggie and Christy must be kept out of it. Nothing must occur which might sever me from them. This time, however, I had mis-understood my mother. Big 'Ina could not cope with the interruptions in her life caused by my escapades. It had been difficult enough while I was a child. Now that I bordered on manhood, she could no longer contain my wildest moments within her life's framework. Rightly, though I thought otherwise at the time, she refused to break up her newly-found contentment and comparative ease, because of the tiresome way I interfered. Most of her youthful years had to be spent slaving for us children and she felt her sacrifice could justifiably end now. Big 'Ina was certainly not going to keep Harry at bay merely because I disliked him. But none of this was clear to me. Had I guessed that for two pins I might have remained in Fermanagh, I should not have left. In the silence I heard war, not peace.

When I arrived in Belfast again, it was to find my place usurped. Believing me to be determined on settling in Fermanagh, Big 'Ina had got another lodger. I could find no place to sleep except on the kitchen hearthrug. I thought this the height of injustice, and callous indifference to the male heir of the family. Summed up in after years, and seen against its proper background, Big 'Ina's action fell completely into line with the way of life in our streets. To survive, you had to be hard. We were the sort of people who called a spade a spade, and no nonsense. My mother had stinted no effort to get me placed in the shipyard. Now that she saw I was determined to stay in the country, she dropped the whole scheme with as much resolve as previously she had taken it up.

At one stage, my future security had seemed to her more important than my present happiness. Perhaps now she dimly perceived that security of her sort could never make me happy. Big 'Ina probably never felt the slightest tinge of jealousy towards Maggie and Christy. At the same time, however, if I arrogated the right to live my own life with them, then she would certainly do the same. My mother doubtless wanted a truce and mutual non-interference. Such thoughts possessed us both, but we spurned discussion, indeed our inner feelings rarely got an airing. So I arrived home, and found myself unwanted. At least some sort of protest could be made. I went upstairs and snatched the eiderdown I had bought, and wrapped myself in it. My night by the sinking, clinking fire was more comfortable than I dared to admit.

Next morning I went to see the Rector, Ould Willie. He alone understood the ins and outs of our turbulent history. He, if anybody, could help me. I badly needed help, not only in this latest of domestic crises, but with my life in general. A clear head was required to sort the tangled threads of difficulties. In spite of a dread that Ould Willie would give me a thorough telling-off, I knocked loudly. But he was all smiles and real concern. Not a word of reproof escaped him because my shadow had not fallen in his church porch since returning from Fermanagh. He concentrated while I poured out my problems. He knew all about Harry, and had already tried to dissuade my elder sister from courting at fourteen. I concluded with the outrage of having to sleep on the kitchen floor. In his wisdom of worldly matters, he saw that I could never fit successfully into the domestic arrangements at home. We were all too confirmed in the new ways of living brought by the war and growing up, ever to change back again. My mother, who had starved to feed and clothe us, could hardly be blamed for liking money now it was available. And I, who had found the independence suited to my nature in the West, could hardly be expected to surrender it. So Ould Willie must have reasoned, and quickly, while I still talked to him. Perhaps others, inexorably changed by war circumstances had perched on the edge of the leather chair in his study, where I sat now. Perhaps in his heart he wept for our vulnerability.

His exterior, however, retained the brisk man-of-action air by which I had always known him. When I finished, his mind was already made up. Something must be done. Like a searchlight probing the sky, his mind sought amongst the alternatives. An apprenticeship where I could live-in occurred to him first. Then he stroked his nose, regarding me critically. Of course, I was tall for my age, and he for one would be proud to see me as a drummer-boy in the Irish Guards. A responsive gleam in my eye not kindled by the idea of apprenticeship, gave him my answer. Without further ado, and busy though he was, Ould Willie devoted the entire day to marching me round the city. When the balloon-chested recruiting sergeant heard the request and my age, he told us I would have to wait some time to be called up. No demand for boys existed. But for Ould Willie 'no' was a word only used in answering the Devil, so an interview with the colonel was fixed. He also could not hasten matters.

It did not mean the end of his search. As I had always wanted to go to sea, an easier settlement lay in that direction. The cabin-boy fiasco of course, did not *really* count as sea-service. The Rector eventually found his way to the director of a leading linen firm. Vested in this august gentleman was the right to approve Ulster candidates for entry to certain British training ships. A plethora of forms showered on me then. I had to fill them in, collect references, and put my finger on the dotted line where Big 'Ina must sign. My mother was delighted, the idea of a sailor-son did not altogether dissatisfy her. A week later I heard they had accepted me. Another form came, a bright yellow one. A tailor had to be found to fill this one in with relevant dimensions—for my uniform! I was down at Weaver to Wearer's by opening time, and had my precious bit of paper completed and away off to the wonder ship. But alas, I must wait until the new term began before the enviable square-rig would be issued to me.

Meanwhile I took another job.

The inevitable interviews at Labour Exchanges, the posting of enquiries to box-numbers, began all over again, and landed me in a hardware and paint merchant's. Two other boys of fourteen started the same morning. Because the boss who interviewed did not turn up, nobody knew where to put us. Within an hour, however, I stood behind the paint counter, transformed by a brown coat into a fully-fledged assistant, with the responsibility of cashing my own sales in the till. It surprised me, the way the other six assistants accepted me as one of themselves and, what was more, the fact that the office goddesses in their silk smocks were willing to date me. No mops of mine hung out of the attic here!

When the blur of faces came into focus and joined themselves to individual characters, I found myself attached to an

The House that Jack Built

English assistant called Jack. Some chord of friendliness vibrated between us. Because he was married, and lived in a cottage in the country, I could look up to him. Jack dressed immaculately, and the pale primrose gloves lent him an air of distinction. His lunch-break and mine coincided, and since he could not go home, as all the others did, he went to restaurants. The elegance of this practice appealed to me, and so I accompanied him. In spite of war-time restrictions, Jack chose his food circumspectly. Bolting buns and eating fish and chips from my hand on the way home, were superseded by sophisticated habits. While we waited for soup, or lingered over our coffee, Jack demonstrated a new use of time for me, a deliberate *rallentando* of the normal working rush. He filled the lunch-hour with talk. Without causing the least embarrassment, he corrected some of my worst table manners. Above all he gave me confidence that I could take my place in a higher social plane without rousing other people's curiosity. I remembered only too well my grand tea above the cinema.

On some days we deliberately hurried over lunch and after eating, went into music shops or Smithfield Market. Music consumed Jack and he had dedicated himself to the violin. This delighted me for one of the finest things in Fermanagh had been Maggie on her fiddle. The mystery of her hard little hands, and the way her work-blunted fingers flew over the strings, had never been solved. Maggie herself scarcely knew how she could clamp turf, milk cows, and an hour afterwards be rolling out a non-stop session of jigs and reels. And expert she was too, at setting our feet going nimbly over the kitchen flagstones.

Jack played no reels. His music had no purpose other than to be beautiful of tone and melody. Once a week he did a fire-watching duty and used it for practising. Those evenings I went to listen, fascinated that the same kind of instrument which Maggie used, could be so different. The practice always began with scales and runs, trills and turns, that threatened occasionally to turn into a jig but never did.

Then Jack would open a piece bought from the piles of sheet music in Smithfield Market. Though not pleased by everything, at least I could distinguish between the Romantic composers and the Classical ones. One piece had a wonderful tune that I learnt from hearing so often. What a surprise I got when he played it with a pianist! Both shared the tune, but in a sort of relay race, first one, then the other leading, and finally, miraculously, ending up together. I looked at the black dots of the music, but they conveyed nothing. How strange to give such stuff, as lively as a running stream, the dull name of *Sonata in A by César Franck*. My demand that it should have a proper name amused Jack. One day he promised to play me a record of five pieces, the first called *Cheerful impressions received on arriving in the country*. He kept his promise, but deceived me, in a way. The sweet music though full of country jigs, bore the terrible, official title *Symphony No. 6 in F, The Pastoral*.

The fact that I would soon be a real sailor was never far from my mind. I was glad of Jack for company because I still could not fit myself in at home. Forgetting my unlikely age, the office girls continued to date me. When wages would allow I took them into a restaurant where perhaps I had lunched with Jack. To swank and show off my familiarity with high living gave me immense satisfaction. Evenings not occupied in that way were often spent with Jack, if he happened to stay in town. Once between supper and the start of fire-watching, we were strolling along, and saw a placard. A famous clairvoyant, said the notice, was holding a séance in the hall. The great medium had come 'direct from

London'. His session had already been on for twenty minutes. Instinctively, I felt what Jack wanted to do.

'Come on!'

Horrified and thrilled, I followed him into the entrance.

While with Jack I seemed to swing violently from one state of mind to another. I never knew what reaction he would provoke next. At one moment he would make me feel like a child ('Don't slouch, Robbie') and the next, especially in front of others, he transformed me into a man (on meeting a friend, 'This is Robert—he's going into the navy'). Now great chunks of solid foundation on which my life was built came away in Jack's hands. Spiritualism! How the word made us shudder as children, when preachers thundered it from pulpits. Spiritualism—worse than the Scarlet Woman of Rome! The haunts of the medium were worse than Catholic chapels. 'Agents of the Devil' were those who tampered with the 'beyond'. Outermost darkness, nethermost pits were reserved for them. Yet in the West I had known, lived with, and even loved Catholics. None had ever tried to murder me. It took much time and heart-searching to see that our preachers had been wrong about Mickeys. Perhaps they were misguided about Spiritualism too. Nevertheless, years of impregnation with anti-medium propaganda could not be forgotten in a moment. The shadow of guilt, the wrath of God, stalked behind me into the hall.

The guilt and the wrath, however, got in for nothing. Jack and I on the other hand, dug in our pockets for milled coins because a plate marked SILVER COLLECTION, appeared under our noses. Two sharp eyes watched closely from a withered potato face, so pale it might itself have belonged to a disembodied spirit. We were in. Only once before had I been so near a seance. Four years or so previously, the gang I belonged to got wind of a meeting. We hoisted each other up to peep over a high windowsill. Whatever dread things we expected to see flying around the room, or whatever orgiastic manifestations, we were disappointed. But what would happen now? Jack still grinned at me, taunting the Protestant reluctance that must have shown in my nervousness. All too often he told me I ought to broaden my outlook. To be on familiar terms with Catholics was apparently not enough.

Except where we squeezed in along the back row, not a seat remained empty. A tense hush amongst the audience shared supremacy with some gooey harmonies. A faint, but distinct odour of human bodies hung in the air. 'Messages' were starting to come in, and people were trying to identify their own dead with the spirit description given. They originated, said Jack, in various 'heavenly planes'. I missed the wicked glint in his eye, the mocking tone in his voice. For him, the whole thing was a bit of a lark. He thought it would do me good to see another side of life. Jack wanted to sweep away the cobwebs of narrowness that still hung in many corners of my mind.

But the séance enthralled me.

A showy young man held the audience. He moved delicately, pacing a small area of platform like a caged tiger. His feet made no sound. Footfalls would surely drive the invisible spirits away. Only the chorus-singing moaned quietly. Once or twice the young man paused. He glanced round swiftly as if a bird brushed against him. Or, and this impressed me, as if a voice spoke in his ear, and his alone. Apparently mistaken, he resumed the restless, nervous pacing. Then suddenly he stood still, clapped a hand to his forehead, spun round, and pointed dramatically down the hall.

The music stopped.

'I have a message for a man in the . . . yes, I think, yes, the back row.' *Our* row!

The House that Jack Built

Floodgates inside me burst, and a tidal wave of half-forgotten emotion swamped me. My father! Of course, the message was for me—surely it was my father calling me. My unhappiness at home had brought him to me. Perhaps he was going to tell me what to do. He must know too that I would soon be a sailor. Tears threatened to shame me. But I could not help remembering the thousand times in childhood when I had spoken to his photograph, so longing for it to answer. Now I would hear his voice.

'The man I want', continued the young medium as I almost shot out of my seat, 'is in the fourth seat.'

Fourth! Mine was only the *second*. Bitter disappointment ran a knife into me. But the man next to Jack did not seem overwhelmed at having a message. In fact he had great difficulty in recognizing anybody he once knew from the medium's description of the spirit. But I felt quite convinced the message *was* for me. Though I could not remember all details about my father, I thought the description fitted well enough. Failing to get a contact from our neighbour, the medium began prancing again, and the wonderful chance of speaking to my father slipped through my fingers.

Jack snorted with amusement at the whole proceedings. He could not know of the awful depression that fell on me. A 'healing circle' followed the first seance, and we stayed on for this. But still no 'message' came through for me. My appetite was thoroughly roused now for occult dabblings. I asked the dried-potato-faced money-collector when the next meeting would be held. He told me to see the secretary of a circle that met privately in the week. They invited me. For the intervening days I moved in a dream, quite absorbed by my new religion.

On the appointed night I found the house, and a group of people in a small room. A naked, red electric bulb gave the only light. We sat in a circle, and after a hymn things happened swiftly. An immensely fat woman from my own side of the city, began groaning and convulsing. Another woman held her hand and spoke comfortingly to her. A young soldier, the faith-healer, played about with her neck. I could not tell whether the departed spirit was conjured out of limbo to deal with the woman's bad throat, but it certainly looked like that. Eventually her convulsions became too violent so the healers treated the patient accordingly. Seen in the subdued, red light, these proceedings produced a hypnotic effect on me. But I was shaken when another spirit informed the circle that an outsider sat in the midst and that his unsympathetic emanations caused difficulties to the spirits. In my excitement over the fat woman I had crossed my legs, giving the astral plane great offence. After all I had been instructed *not* to do this, but to sit like a Victorian child, knees together and hands resting on them. However, I enjoyed it all, especially the bits where spirits demanded a song like *Roses Round the Door* instead of choruses. Sometimes the spirits cracked jokes which made us all laugh. We got our money's worth on that evening, for it was quite late when the healers stopped roaming about, groping. All that had to be done then was the slapping back to normality of those women who had gone into advanced 'states', and the singing of the group's signature tune, *Bringing in the sheaves*.

Jack's view-broadening over Spiritualism took greater effect than he originally intended. He had wanted me to mock it, and rid myself of a prejudice. Instead I took it seriously, although I never told him how seriously. The other interests were enough to cope with, especially the dining out. In spite of the restricted meals allowed by the war, Jack hunted down many interesting places to eat. Going to restaurants every lunch-time and most evenings would have been far beyond my beginner's wage in spite of the war-time five-shilling limit on cost. But I had sidelines. In Fermanagh the trapping had given me a taste for a private income. Rabbits could not be caught in Belfast, but I found other ways of money-making.

At the hardware shop, morning tea-break occurred at eleven o'clock, and we had to provide our own cups. I invaded my precious tin trunk full of the 'posh'—the china I collected while living with Maggie. A large and suitably strong cup that came from a country mansion, seemed ideal. No sooner had its rich royal blues and gilded arabesques appeared among its cracked and handleless companions in the kitchen, than one of the girls fell in love with it. A girl called Sadie was in charge of the tea-making, and because she was getting married soon, asked if she could have the cup. War demands increasing every day, left no time for the making of china as fine as mine. My most treasured pieces had already gone back to the farm—in our own house china was far too handy as a missile during rows and fights. Now I was very pleased to part with a set of cups and saucers for five times the price I paid originally. Once the others discovered the market, they all wanted things for themselves or friends. A considerable part of the collection vanished in a short time with similar profit to me.

Another activity brought me handsome rewards. It was by no means an uncommon one, but less reputable than selling china. People could manage without Staffordshire cups, but few could live the daily round with no clothes. And in those rationed days, this meant clothing coupons. Some families devoured them, and coupons were more valuable to them than bank-notes. Like hundreds of men in hundreds of pubs, and hordes of women in teashops, I *knew someone* who could get me coupons, which for a price, I would let anyone have,

My source was a humble but steady one. Several large families lived near Maggie, and they always seemed to be in need of clothes. But for financial reasons they preferred second-hand ones from lorries in the fair to new clothes, and I was always being implored to send cast-offs from our house. On the rare occasions when the families decided new clothes were essential, they liked to go across the border and buy them in war-free Eire. So their coupon books arrived for me. Maggie and Christy added most of theirs also, for neither felt a need for new clothes. Gradually the number of my customers grew, some of them appearing on the sweet-coupon list too. I made inroads on the collection of sweet coupons myself. Every time I took a girl to see *Mrs. Miniver* a bar of chocolate helped to stem the tears. At work we kept a record of individual attendances at this film. Everybody had been at least twice, and indulged in the copious weeping that was thought highly patriotic.

Sadie's difficulty in finding furniture for her new home set me on another venture. I had always been a handyman, and under Christy's tuition learnt quite a few tricks of carpentry and joinery. Before long l was turning out furniture reclaimed from markets and junk shops. The sight of a good rosewood table going for firewood for a few shillings offended my sense of economy. How easy it was to remove the filth on top and repolish it. Rescued bookcases responded in a similar way, when wire-brushed to remove caked dirt and cracked varnish. White paint smeared into the grain of the exposed natural wood caught the fancy of girls getting married. They even got me to hang paper for them.

Together, these industries and businesses made me wealthy and independent compared with most boys of fourteen. The only threat to my income came from a little man who french-polished my masterpieces of furniture. I supplied him with methylated spirits for his work. He always called for it when Jack and I were alone at the paint counter between twelve and one o'clock. A detective came in one day wanting to see the names of those who signed the book for methylated spirits. This caused me alarm as the old polisher never signed for his, because he said he could not write. Until that moment I had not realized to what uses, other than french-polishing, methylated spirits could be put by dipsomaniacs.

Perhaps the greatest results of my money were in changes at home. I could afford to give the whole of my shop wage to my mother, receiving in return the sole use of my old room —without the lodgers. Good terms prevailed between Big 'Ina and myself at that moment. When the lodger who had occupied my room was taken to prison, owing several weeks' rent, she presented me with his watch. But a major battle succeeded the peace, over a lock I fixed on my door, not so much to close it as to symbolize my independence. The row ended by my rushing out to the police barracks for reinforcements.

With a room of my own again, friction with the family worried me less. I willingly set about converting the place from a dingy hole into a smart bed-sitting-room. As though stripping the dead past from my life. I pulled off the old wallpaper, with its hardly distinguishable pink ribbons tied round bunches of violets, long since faded. Certainly after my father's death eight years previously, we could not afford redecoration. Whistling in my tuneless way, I worked round the room, recalling childhood incidents as each piece came away in my hands. In its place I was going to put on a coat of light dove-grey that would show up my Paul Henry reproductions.

This painter's luminous skies, and clouds flying before a west wind off the Atlantic, evoked deep feelings in me. His thousand blues and purples shaded soft mountains with the mystery I knew they had in reality. How many times had I climbed Fermanagh's hills and flung myself down in the heather. How many shadows had I watched chasing patches of sun across the rolling landscape. How many times had I lifted my head from working in the fields to feel the wind veering, bringing the smell of rain. I could not number them. All you ever smelt in Belfast was factory smoke and traffic fumes. Now Paul Henry's soft brush and blue-toned pictures served to keep my affections fixed where they belonged—in the West.

Artists who follow realism, and paint what they think they see, can hardly blame people for seeing the picture not the art. For me Paul Henry reminded me of the West better than any other artist. Whether his art was better or worse did not worry me. Another Paul, however, was to rouse my interest in art proper. Jack gave me two Gauguin reproductions for a Christmas present. Of course I was not articulate on the effect they had on me. All I knew was that a sultry vitality glowed in his paintings, entirely missing from Paul Henry's. The new Paul had so much more to convey, and I became aware that it lay in the picture itself, not in the subject portrayed.

Paul Gauguin's shadowless world, his dark-souled people with over-large eyes and bacon-slice lips, the exotic vegetable growths they moved among, were obviously not *real*. You couldn't get on a boat in Belfast and sail off, and find a country and people who *looked* like that. Yet Gauguin and his weird forms worked such magic that I *felt* as if I lay sweltering in jungles, or rode bareback along shell-pink tropical beaches. And I knew Gauguin conjured his spell by colour alone. How rich his reds and chromes glowed on my wall beside the cool, watery Paul Henry. I could not guess then that one day I would taste for myself Gauguin's emotions, on numerous hibiscus shores. Perhaps every Saxon, every Viking, every

Celt, has a dream of a tropical island burning deep in his primitive soul. I had. And Gauguin kindled my desire to see the tropics, that before many months turned into flames that consumed the whole of my life.

Meanwhile a Celt I must remain, for on turning from my pictures, I looked out over the slate roofs and the railway lines. If temporarily I must belong to the city, then I would take the pleasures it offered. Again to Jack I owed my new consciousness of clothes. He eyed critically anything of mine that sagged, bagged, or came too short on my lanky limbs. After more than a few hints, I went to a tailor for a good suit. Because turn-ups were banned by war regulations, I asked the assistant to make the trousers a few inches too long, so that I could turn them up myself. The suit had to be ready, I told him, for a very special occasion. I omitted to explain that this was the Christmas party of Mavis's Christian Endeavour group. For Mavis was the girl from the office on whom I finally settled.

Mavis scarcely played Isolde to my Tristan, for she was alas, only a second best. Of course I did not tell her that my longings reached out in the black of wakeful nights for Sadie, the girl with whom I actually worked. But as Sadie was engaged, almost spliced, and had half her home already collected, including my cups and some of my furniture restorations, she lay beyond my grasp—even, and this frustrated me more than anything, beyond my embrace. So Mavis would have to do. She did in fact quite well. I am not sure now whether half the romance about her lay in my thinking what *might* happen, rather than what actually came to pass. Human nature abhors a vacuum, and Mavis amply filled the emptiness that occurred in my mind when it was not engaged with paint and putty during working hours, and food, Spiritualism or Sadie, in my free time.

The House that Jack Built

Mavis was consumed by a passion unfortunately not for me, but for her ambition to be a lay preacher. To this end she spent most of her evenings at study classes. No amount of tempting offers from me about seeing *Mrs. Miniver* in the most expensive cinema's best seats could sway her. The classes must go on. Eventually it turned out that if I wanted Mavis, then I would have to go where she was. In this way I was assured at least of one regular, and whole, evening with her each Tuesday. A slight disadvantage existed because this had to be shared in company with thirty other people, at the principal weekly meeting of the Christian Endeavour. The cold hall, the hard chairs, the naked lights, and green baize tables, might be thought inconducive to love-making. But my whole childhood had been lived against the background of such meetings. I hardly noticed that the atmosphere differed totally, for instance, from Gauguin's islands. And anyway, after the meeting I walked Mavis home. Love had the Midas touch.

Mavis liked me to walk her home whenever possible, on evenings other than Tuesdays. She was afraid of being alone in the black-out streets, not because of an inverted wish that she might be attacked, but because of spies. Mavis felt entirely convinced that German agents shadowed her. Before coming to the hardware firm, Mavis had worked as a personal secretary to a director. Then suddenly he disappeared off to Dublin and was never seen again. And we all knew Dublin was a hot-bed of German spies. The idea obsessed Mavis, and she struggled to recall juicy titbits from overheard telephone conversations which might incriminate her old boss. Even when I went with her, Mavis flew off at high speed if a dim figure in the black-out appeared to be following us. At times I was almost convinced myself, especially if somebody turned off behind us through a side street.

Twice Mavis baked a mountain of scones and tarts to which Sadie and her fiancé were invited, along with me. Seemliness rather than abandonment dominated the entertainment that followed the food—Happy Families. As we flipped our way through Mr. Fin the Fishmonger and Mr. Bun the Baker, I could not suppress a thought which sneaked in that despite the combined attractions of Sadie and Mavis, a good *ceili* at Maggie's with the dancing and laughing would have made a far finer evening.

The glittering pinnacle to this structure of evenings spent in Christian joy, would be the Endeavour's Christmas party. Hence my suit, which I planned should be ready some days beforehand. But of course it wasn't. I went to the tailor's twice a day, as though my personal appearance would make the stitches go in faster. Not until the very evening of the party did the tailor hold out the hanger with the beautiful creation suspended on it. In order to arrive on time at Mavis's rather grand suburb, I changed into my suit at the back of the shop. Somehow my feet did not seem to emerge from the trouser-legs. Of course, the turn-ups! I had forgotten the extra length allowed for these. It was too late now to convert them. All I could do was hitch the trousers up as far as they would go. Luckily I still wore my wireless aerial to continue the good work of straightening my shoulders. Now I unwound it feverishly, and rewound it to my ribs, holding the trousers as high as possible. The fine new jacket slipped comfortably on to my shoulders, covering the aerial-bound trousers.

A glowing Mavis received me, and from her comments I knew the suit had made its mark. The party followed the typical evangelical pattern—tea and tame sandwiches followed by gormless games of a *The Farmer Wants a Wife* genus. During one such game, the females formed up in four lines for team races round a chair at the hall's farther end. The distinguishing feature of this hilarious fun, however, was that the women runners had to wear a man's jacket turned inside out. While the awful truth sunk in, I saw Mavis heading in my direction. What, oh what, would be said about my hitched trousers, and the aerial? I felt Mavis's fingers on my buttons already.

'Mavis,' I said, 'I'm not feeling well. Take me outside.'

Neither was I indeed, though not, as Mavis thought, because something in the sandwiches was 'off'.

CHAPTER VII

Gospel Belles

Y ou could easily see how Mavis differed from Sadie. Her hair, for instance, coarse and sandy, was disciplined into the current page-boy fashion. 'Forced' might be a better word than 'disciplined'. At the other extremity a similar hairy effect obtained from her feet. Stout legs disappeared into equally stout boots. These were fur ones, bald and shiny about the ankles where they rubbed together. Perhaps her post as deputy-pianist at the Christian Endeavour meetings, precluded a more eye-catching ensemble. And Mavis of course was a typist at the hardware and paint merchant's.

Compare Sadie.

True she held the position as honorary treasurer of the Gospel Tract Band, and her husband-to-be acted as secretary to the Missionary Prayer Letter. But these high ecclesiastical achievements could not disguise the fact that in the shop Sadie weighed out lowly putty and filled bottles with humble turpentine. Alas—Sadie even had no shorthand. But I cared about none of it. Sadie could even have scrubbed the floors, and I would have worshipped her not a heartache less. Her face appeared in my mind as a constant image. Indeed even when she was not there I could see her skin, so milky-white against the raven hair. Under her eyes, the pure skin was so delicately stencilled as to give her a plaintive, pleading expression—the fey look which shattered my soul. In spite of the large spaniel eyes, and the dreaming vagueness that swam in them, her face did not rely on them. I often thought her most beautiful during the morning tea-break, when the eyes were closed while she muttered a grace to herself.

How I tortured myself thinking of Nirvana, of being absorbed into supreme bliss. But it was quite unattainable for me—Sadie's wedding date was already fixed. There was no need for *me* to enquire for whom the bells were tolling. Consumed with passion, whispering her name to the moon, writing her notes and poems which I immediately tore up, that was my lot. Strictly in the best, tragic manner, my love burned brighter as time went on. But no fulfilment other than staring quite rudely at her, would ever be mine. What subtlety, as delicately shaded as a charcoal drawing, eluded me about that face? I never knew. Perhaps Spanish blood mingled long ago from a wrecked Armada galleon, mingled in her veins. Perhaps at that time my own blood was too fevered from looking at Gauguin's immobile, throbbing figures.

Strangely, like so many evangelical women, God had gifted the 'saved' Sadie with a most generous bust. This also attracted me, the effect of it and the face combined shot me down, as the phrase then was, in flames. Bosoms were laid on these religious women almost like crosses. Certainly they regarded them as deformities and did their utmost to submerge them. Some buttoned themselves up to the chin, while others stretched a camouflage of out-dated modesty vest across the gap so sinfully left by godless dressmakers. Cities on hills, however, cannot be hid. Sadie's profile, especially around the thorax, caused more mistakes in my cash register than any-thing else.

Added to my love-pains, was the knowledge that Sadie bore an interest in me too. Inexperience led me to think this a far less spiritual matter than actually was the case. I suppose, partly, I was ready to lap up any kind of interest. True, Sadie had a penchant for my cups and saucers, and by my extra coupons I could play on her sweet tooth. Yet her fundamental concern lay in my soul. I had asked for trouble in this direc-tion by blabbing about the séances I went to—'Devil's meet-ings'.

And here Sadie joined forces with Mavis. Though both girls confessed to being 'born again', in the normal course of events, they were not in common communion. Sadie be-longed to a 'pure' sect, that had come 'right out of the world'. Actually they had originally come right out of the Baptist persuasion, though not holding that 'taking the waters' was essential to membership and the Sabbath breaking-of-bread. This sect spurned Mavis's and its badminton club, and its 'modern' Methodists' Saturday rambles—as though they were the veritable garlic and cucumbers of Egypt. Sadie's sect scorned the need of exercise. If young limbs wanted to release surplus energy, they could take part in street parades with scriptural sandwich-boards, or in open-air witness. A multitude of ways existed by which to serve the Lord, with-out knocking shuttlecocks round a room. In any case the girls of Mavis's group wore shorts. And although nobody in Sadie's sect had ever looked on such a thing since 'conver-sion', everybody knew that they showed too much leg. Nevertheless, though strict to the law's letters, Sadie saw no crime in stealing away to join Mavis in a quiet part of the warehouse. Amongst the crates the girls united in prayer for my deliverance from Spiritualism.

Worse was to follow. Mavis resorted to violence when the effects of prayer were not forthcoming. She threatened to give me up altogether if I refused to be 'saved'. This on its own might not have had much effect on me. But what one girl could do, so might another. I would die surely if Sadie denied me her friendship, regrettably platonic though it was. I thought of a long vista of days behind the paint-counter, where never a ray of sunshine from the spaniel eyes fell, of the awful silence that would engulf me if we did not have our tea together. Sandy-haired Mavis would not be missed much—but Sadie, it would be outer darkness indeed without her. Anyway, the dice were loaded, so what alternative had I?

Christmas came and went after the awful party. January set in again with winds blowing raw from all directions at once. A feeble powdering of snow appeared on roofs and the tops of post-boxes on some mornings, but vanished by midday. This was the period for renewal of hope before the coming spring—souls included. Sadie's sect held its annual mission at this time of the year. Each 'brother' and 'sister' had to bring an unconverted soul to hear a famous evangelist. Every night of the week saw meetings being held, with sessions of prayer for believers to precede them.

A request-box stood at the back of the hall. Slips of paper were dropped in by the faithful, bearing the names and histories of sinners and 'backsliders' on whom they had fixed their talons. The prayer-group riffled through these, no doubt dealing with the juiciest specimens first. Sadie put my case in the box, and the group got down to seeking my day of grace. I could even bear this if only it meant maintaining my slender thread of contact with Sadie. I could even stand belonging to the group which had no badminton or Saturday rambles, if only Sadie still hovered on my horizon.

Trapped, I made my promise to attend the mission. Mavis

all agog for my salvation (I would then be respectable enough
to meet her family) readily agreed to accompany us. Though
quite a well-known centre, I had never been in this particular
hall before. But it made no difference. Our trio hardly got in
the doors before I was recognized instantly. The people who
patronized that sort of thing had a kind of inverted snobbery
over moral matters. The worse you were, the more they
esteemed you after 'conversion'. The more filthy your
language, the more dreadful your drunkenness, the more
wild with women you were, the more they prized you.
What enjoyable public confessions of all these sins could be
squeezed out of you, what vicarious tasting of the Devil's
delights. But the capture of one who practised the black art,
and had been in personal communication with Lucifer himself—what a sensational acquisition for the congregation!

Everyone in the place knew what kind of sinner Sadie was
to bring. Seeing me with her, they drank their fill of sin un-
repentant. When the evening was over, I would be 'saved'—
no longer an object of curiosity. Audiences in the Roman
arenas must have looked in such a way at gladiators before
they were slaughtered. Sadie showed no embarrassment at
being the centre of attention. She introduced her family who
spoke kindly to me. They used a kind of courtesy which
meant that before long I would be one of them. But what an
agony to shake the stranger's hand and hear 'I'm praying for
you.'

We went inside and took our places. I knew perfectly what
would follow, for I was no foreigner to Gospel meetings,
missions and the like. Largely because other forms of entertainment were rare or too expensive, since the age of three I
had regularly attended these conventicle services. All had
been of every possible permutation on the basic creed. The
raising of a hand in public, by the individual sinner, as being

a token of having asked 'Christ into the heart', was the crux of the whole matter. As a young boy I had even raised my own hand, though only as a bet. I won a slab of toffee for this from a friend who dared me. But that hand-raising I knew well did not count, for afterwards I still went to the cinema, and chased the girls up the entries.

However, continuous indoctrination through eleven of my most impressionable years was bound to leave deep marks. Superficial though I might have been, the merciless reiteration of a few simple tenets, sank into my mind, whether I would or no. At no identifiable point in my life I took it for granted that one day, somewhere, far away in the future, I would have to be 'born again'. Everybody did, just like leaving school and starting work, just like courting and getting married. Those who put off the day of salvation never went to heaven —just as those who didn't work never had enough to eat, or those who didn't open their parlour curtains never had a three-piece suite. The only thing was, you tried to put off the day of grace as long as possible.

So much had happened to me, it seemed, since I departed from Maggie in the height of Fermanagh's summer. Manhood and responsibility dropped on me like well-made cloaks. I earned my own living and already 'went' with a girl. And in any case, we Belfast boys knew from the moment we entered school that when the miraculous age of fourteen was reached we would be transformed into men. Further procrastination was obviously impossible for me now. All events conspired together, stars moved in their courses, to prove that this was the moment when I must be 'saved'. Although I knew it must happen one day, I had so hoped to grow quite old first. In younger years I loved smoking cigarette butts and going to football matches—things you couldn't do after you 'met the Lord'.

Alternative theology to that of the Gospel halls came from the Church of Ireland. Because it supported me during most of my childhood, I had attended its services also, besides the mission-halls'. But the atmosphere differed completely. It had a real churchy touch, quiet, solemn and dim. Nobody threatened us with lakes of fire and gnashing of teeth. No question of getting 'saved' ever came up. Sadie and I had already held lengthy arguments as to why in her view episcopalians were not Christians, through not being 'saved'. John 3: 16 was the evangelicals' gospel in a nutshell—they cracked it at every gathering. On the other hand, I upheld the Apostle's Creed to Sadie as the touchstone on which to decide who was, or was not, Christian. Our Rector, and even I myself, I said, were as much Christians as she. Sadie would have none of this. How could we be? No hands had gone up in a meeting, therefore Christ was not our *personal* Saviour. Q.E.D.

Slowly my grip loosened. I could not deny that Sadie would have been far less attractive had she been a swearer, a gambler, a chaser of men. Mavis also, whom I *could* take as a girl-friend, would not have been worth looking at twice, had she not possessed the air of dignity-cum-innocence which appealed to me. There would certainly be no harm in getting 'born again'. It was the business of doing it in public that was nauseous and faintly obscene. My flirtation with Spiritualism made no obstacle. Having witnessed most of its spectacular carryings-on, I threw it over. Nobody ever received messages of any significance, and I not a single one from my father. A letter from Fermanagh finally turned me against it. Maggie had been really heart-broken when I wrote to her about the séances. She who believed so dearly in charms, was horrified that I wanted to get in touch with my father, and implored me never to go again.

And so in this way, by slow degrees, my salvation became inevitable.

I looked forward to it gravely, as I had regarded the start of my career in the shipyard. Being 'saved' like being a working-man, might hold unforeseen pleasures or sadnesses. None could tell. But it had to be done, and I prepared myself accordingly. Never, for one moment, did I question the validity of the whole ritual. I never doubted that God was in His heaven, along with Jesus and the Holy Ghost, and that when my hand went up at the meeting, an angel would seize a golden pen and print ROBERT HARBINSON on the outsize guest-book kept by God for the occasion, the Book of Life. The only uncertain element had been myself. Now, however, I was sure.

The two girls and I came to the hall materially reinforced by an after-closing time meal in the office. Mavis had baked some of her delicious, feathery pastry and served a fine tea. There was no time to go home before the mission began—or at least, the girls wanted to keep me within eye-shot for fear of last-minute recantation. Three nights of the mission had gone already, producing eight converts, so that the whole thing was a roaring success.

We left the office, and my hand (the one shortly to be raised) was wrung by strong evangelical grips, and we entered the hall, Sadie on my right, Mavis on the left. Sadie's mother whispered as we sidled into a row, 'The Lord is working.' Tears welled in Sadie's eyes. I sensed that other people in the hall knew we had arrived, but their glances were brief, if noticeable at all. I tried to look penitent and humble. On each side of me the girls bent their heads in prayer. Nothing so sharp as a knife would have been needed to cut the atmosphere. Not wishing at this of all times to be odd man out, I too leant over. Unfortunately the back of the

bench in front had a two-way hinge, like a tram seat. As the
people in it were also leaning forwards, the back-rest swung
under my heavy movement. A loud protest of un-oiled
metal rang round the room. I wanted to giggle and com-
pressed my mouth. A glimpse of the tears in Sadie's abstracted
eyes checked this before I made a spectacle of myself. The
girls had lost no time in battling for my soul. But all I could
wish was that they would sit up straight, so we could start on
the liquorice allsorts—Sadie's favourite.

The meeting proper would not begin for some minutes
and meanwhile I had a good look round. People considered
that particular hall an elegant structure. None of the usual
corrugated iron and wood could be found about this place,
but solid brick, spaced with generous windows full of frosted
glass. A plaster ceiling decorated with foliated bosses from
which hung green-burning lamps, gave the place a luxurious
character. No aisle ran between benches and wall, and the
ends were already well packed, for the gas radiators hissed
quietly there. Self denial did not extend to stoic practices. All
these things were mere details compared with the hall's main
feature, the platform. The preacher's reading desk and the
armchairs for the elders comprised its furnishings. What fascinated me most was a brass balustrade at the front edge. A
hairy green curtain on brass rings like gipsy's ear-rings, was
drawn across it. The idea presumably being to allow the
elders' legs to cross and uncross without distracting the congregation from 'the message'. At similar affairs, it had always
filled moments of boredom to see the different socks the
elders wore, and sometimes, suspenders too. Tonight,
naturally, there would be no boredom.

Gradually the place filled, the elders filed on to the platform, with the special evangelist conducting the mission. I
noticed his spats and very grand cravat. As soon as he started

talking, his Adam's apple bobbed up and down. It rode
between the wings of an unusually high 'come-to-Jesus' collar,
like a buoy during choppy weather out in the Lough. And, of
course, the size of Bible he carried matched the trumpet-
toned reading. He was good at it. In spite of his age, the fire
of a melodrama actor flamed from him. Even his eyebrows
expressed terror or hope, by quivering up or fluttering down.
At intervals he slapped his Bible shut, and went on his knees,
rocking to and fro, to demonstrate the agony of those in hell,
who had heard 'the message' but denied it. He varied this by
allowing his voice to die softly away altogether. Then noises
from the street at the back would filter through, laughter and
voices of the 'unsaved' going by to perdition, and the clang of
passing trams, measuring the tide-mark of eternity.

Then the evangelist swung round on one heel, a terrible
expression on his face. A masterly finger pointed to the
decorated ceiling. A taut silence stretched across the room like
a drum-skin. It seemed as though the gas stopped hissing, and
as if even the trams were halted. Slowly the hand came down.
In a voice no louder than cricket's chirping he said, spacing
his words, 'The . . . Lord . . . may . . . come. . . .' Then the
voice took on power, louder, farther-reaching, seeking out
every hidden dust-choked crevice in the room. Did not the
'unsaved' there tonight, realize that within the hour, the
Lord might come? He might appear in glory at the trumpet's
ring. Death, he went on, trembling at the clarion clearness of
his own oration, death within the hour might stalk the 'unsaved' down, taking them off the face of the earth, all chance
of heaven forfeited. Could we reject even at this late hour, the
Lord's calling? Could we fail to put up our hand?

Could we?

Well no, all things considered, we could not. The coming
of the Lord had been a terrible thing in my childhood. Such

threats as the evangelist made in common with his kind, cut such wounds in my infant breast, that I briefed my little sister with doom-drill. As soon as she heard the angel's trumpet, I told her, she must fall on her knees and cry out to be 'saved'. It would, I imagined, be something like the air-raid siren sounding the alert. This used to be the trump-card I held up my own sleeve—until the day when somebody kindly pointed out, that the descending Christ was not going to stop in mid-flight just to rub out *my* sins from the Book of Life, I, the prince of sinners, who had robbed our own gas-meter and pee'd in the cemetery!

Wearing sinners down by sheer weight of words, the preacher wound the meeting up like a clockwork mouse. At any minute now, the spring would be released, and the wheels fly round. Who takes the Lord Jesus into his or her heart as their personal Saviour? When we got to that point, I felt quite convinced of the need for this personal witness. In my own fashion I had always been fundamentally religious for as long as I could remember, certainly believing the man Jesus Christ to be my own, in addition to being the Saviour of the world.

My hand went up. I did not make it. It just went up of its own accord, as if seized by an ataxic spasm. I could not have pulled it down at that moment if I had wanted to. My hand hung there, like a flag on a rifle-range showing that a bull had been scored. Immediately a clamour started among the congregation. 'Praise the Lord' they began, first one, then several together, and finally the whole in chorus.

The service came quickly to an end. They ushered me into a prayer-room with Mavis and Sadie. An elderly woman, perhaps the evangelist's wife, came too, and joined in praying with the girls, while the preacher flicked over the India paper pages of his Bible, to remove all lingering doubts. But I could not listen properly as the women were now thoroughly tear-bound, and I considered that something of the sort was expected from me. And I found it impossible to look straight at the evangelist, for despite the spats and fine dickey, and his endless use of long words, his breath smelt. Instead, I stretched a hand across the table, and nervously twitched at some gaudy paper roses.

'Jesus, Rose of Sharon,' cried the preacher.

The elderly woman started a very weird rendering of,

> *'By cool Siloam's shady rill*
> *How sweet the lily grows!*
> *How sweet the breath, beneath the hill,*
> *Of Sharon's dewy rose!'*

Sadie's family and other well-wishers waited outside, as though for election results. Once more my hand was shaken by all in sight (my poor hand, it had not done so much work in one evening since the last harvest at Maggie's) and Sadie introduced me as *Robert*—no more Robbies, Bobs, or Long-legs, because I was 'Christian' now. Next morning at work the assistant manager himself came out of the office and into the paint department, specially to shake my hand and call me 'brother'. Then came the arrival of suitable presents to mark this giant occasion in my two lives—the one here on earth and that in the hereafter. They gave me *Daily Light*, the music version of *Sacred Songs and Solos*, Cruden's *Concordance*, Bogatsky's *Golden Treasury*, and a promise-box from Mavis.

Tiny rolls of paper, standing on end, made the inside of the promise-box like the wax cells of a honeycomb. In size the rolls resembled those in Christmas crackers, but instead of mottos bore Scriptural promises. As if the box contained the choicest crystallized fruits, a roll was selected or offered to friends, to taste delights promised in the Book.

Gospel Belles

Sadie gave me a badge for my lapel. Though small, the words it bore stood out clearly—JESUS SAVES. It was a great sign of unafraid witness and shielded the wearer from bad language and spicy stories, for sinners tended to respect it. Afterwards, I sometimes changed a jacket before going out, but forgot to transfer the badge. Sadie would notice it immediately. Her reprimand would hardly have been sharper had I gone out without trousers.

Before a week elapsed, my life changed. A host of new activities so crowded my free hours, that even had I wanted to drink, smoke, gamble, no time would have been found. My new 'sisters' enrolled me in the Scripture Union. A booklet of daily notes was issued to be read in conjunction with a passage in the Bible. *Daily Light* could be read in bed in the morning, but the Union 'portions' were usually studied later in the day with Sadie. Given luck, we might sneak round the back of the warehouse, and have a really lovely little time of fellowship.

Like a circus, the mission was a seven-day wonder. For the remainder of that week we attended it, I crying in my turn, 'Praise the Lord' at new 'conversions'. The closing Sunday blazed with triumph. We spent the entire day at the hall, except when parading with banners through the streets. The struggles of a St. Anthony or a St. Jerome were not to be mine, for I took to salvation like fish to water. Somehow, now that the thing was accomplished, a great worry was lifted from my mind. Almost in sheer relief, I was willing to do anything, go anywhere, that might be demanded. Part of the newly 'saved's' obligations involved confession at the open-air meetings of past sins. This was called giving your 'testimony'. The worst sins, of course, made the best 'testimony'. Already I was urged to indulge in this public speaking. On the mission's final night, the week's converts had to write out their 'testimonies' and put them in a box. Then the visiting evangelist picked them out on the platform one by one, to read them aloud. During this recitation of crime, the convert had to stand up. I wondered if my single paragraph of confession would be considered sufficient. It took the preacher half a minute to go through it. But his exegesis on the hellish evils of Spiritualism went on and on. Even the most hardened evangelical bottoms began to shift on the benches in discomfort.

The mission concluded exactly a week before I was due to cross The Water to join my training ship. This plan for my future had been opposed by Sadie from the start. In my vanity, I hoped that her objection was at the thought of losing *me*. I misjudged her spiritual fervour, for it was nothing of the sort. Refusing to deal herself with my imminent departure, she laid the problem before an elder. He gave me a heart-to-heart. I was too young in the faith to face temptations in the Forces. I must learn to walk before I could run. The old man felt convinced that I would soon omit my prayers. Would I not be afraid of saying them before getting into my hammock, because of being laughed at? He had known so many youngsters fail on joining the Forces, from just that cause. No—my proposed navy career should not be taken lightly. I must devote myself to serious prayer, seeking the Lord's guidance about my life. In my public 'testimony', he said encouragingly, I had shown great promise, and he had little doubt but that the Lord held great things in store, and intended to use me powerfully.

I could not fail to be immensely impressed and not a little flattered by his earnestness and concern. Back at home, in my room, I felt torn apart, and could make no decision. The training ship lure, prelude to adventure on the high seas, seemed irresistible. Furthermore, it had my mother's backing.

She saw the means in it not only of getting me over a difficult age, but also of my learning a trade—still, in her mind the key to security. On the other side of this tug-o'-war, the evangelicals also pulled weightily. Sadie's personal appeal was not the least influence among them. Many times a day I plundered the promise-box. But it gave equivocal answers, and seemed quite as unable to make up its mind as I was. I had only to extract a tiny roll bearing the words *My presence shall go with thee*, to read in it confirmation of my navy career. But the next might contain the word 'rest', and this I interpreted as an indication that I was to stay with Sadie behind the paint-counter. On looking for a sign, I found none. Waiting on the Lord apparently required superhuman patience.

On Wednesdays a fellowship meeting took place. Besides lengthy explanations on Biblical texts, they dealt in a musical side-line too. Male voice choirs often came to sing the better kind of hymn to W. H. Jude's settings. On other occasions big women warbled with contralto voices that had roots in their boots. But on the Wednesday preceding my week-end departure for the ship, Sadie was our soloist. Her voice was a rill of sweetness that quite offset her shakiness on top notes. And it was not merely her voice, and the delicately-coloured face, the pleading eyes, and her indefinable Hispano-Tahitan air that moved me. This time, I got the answer about my future, for the hymn's words went like an arrow into my heart. Surely she selected that hymn because of me—

> *Brightly beams our Father's mercy*
> *From his lighthouse evermore;*
> *But to us He gives the keeping*
> *Of the lights along the shore.'*

Yes, Sadie would keep the land-lights, and trim my own

'feeble lamp'. It was now impossible to desert her for the navy.

The accursed papers from the training ship were destroyed, and a rude letter sent off, enclosing a Gospel tract. Sadie and I had a fine time of thanksgiving up in the paint store-room.

CHAPTER VIII

Savings Campaign

Neither with world, flesh, nor Devil could there now be any compromise. The sinner's wilderness of drink and tobacco, cinema and theatres, dances and billiards, was unthinkable. Even the general field of reading was excluded. Once, but only once, I made a great *faux pas* by quoting Shakespeare when giving my 'testimony'. The temperature in the hall seemed to drop several degrees, and I finished my speech in confusion, frozen by the awful expression from the faithful. This lesson was salutary. I returned all my tickets to the public library, for only books obtained from the Bible depot down town were considered 'pure'. Further purchases of literary magazines to which Jack introduced me, were banned, and remaining copies burnt. If I wanted a quiet session in the warehouse lavatory now, it had to be with the *Christian Herald*.

Gauguin's bodies were stripped from the walls of my bedroom and hidden away. Instead I nailed up a reproduction of *The Broad and Narrow Way*. As art, it reached a low level. But as a picture with a story to tell it could hardly have been bettered. That I liked it, was fortunate, because the next seven years of my life were destined to be flavoured by its lurid colouring. The moral pointed was simple and aimed at simple people. Two roads wound up from the foreground, to end in their respective dramatic climaxes—one in death and damnation, the other in life and salvation. And those two alternatives, we believed, confronted every human being. Mankind must choose.

Contained in the picture, working their way up from the bottom to top, were scores of little figures. The extreme gravity of the subject matter, however, lost a little in dignity because the tiny painted men and women were all dressed in Victorian clothes, complete with bustles and bonnets, top-hats and frock-coats. Most evangelicals were familiar with the population of *The Broad and Narrow Way*—a population, it seemed, composed largely of the well-to-do.

Life being what it is, and presumably, was, very few could be seen on the Narrow Way to salvation. This may have been because its entrance lay through a barely noticeable wicket-gate by a neo-Gothic church. Once through, the way proved to be a very mean affair indeed. It passed the red brick Sunday School, the Gospel Tent, the rustic cottage called *Talitha Cumi*, and the Deaconess Institution. Beyond this small town the figures became even fewer on the mountain track which led to heaven. A dear old, shawled lady held back her son while a Roman soldier fought a lion. The last person visible on the track was very indistinct. You could just discern that he had fallen in thanksgiving on his knees before the golden gates, like a bullfrog springing to mate. The first reward awaiting the pilgrim was a pair of palm branches and a crown copied from the British regalia. Last of all came the decidedly dreary-looking New Jerusalem. Similar architectural monstrosities crowded its streets as littered the track below. Above it, like a cod on a slab, strict files of angels flew, blowing trumpets.

What a different proposition was the Broad Way of Perdition. So many more exciting things happened along it, that crowds could not be blamed for wandering in. Besides, its gate was wide and bore a large sign WELCOME. Who could resist that, especially as Venus and Bacchus held the sign. Things started at once. The gate-lodge, for instance, was inhabited by a lively little wench, seducing a youth in a bowler hat, beckoning him to the 'lips of honeycomb' and the bed perfumed with 'myrrh, aloes and cinnamon'. Behind the harlot stood the Theatre Royal, and nearby an old gent leaning on a cane. Two lads had just picked his pockets.

Villainy occupied many of the Broad Way people. One man whipped his fallen donkey without mercy, youths engaged in fisticuffs, bandits sprang out of bushes with rifles, gangs of chained prisoners went miserably by, red-tuniced soldiers were 'on the job', old roués made eyes at the girls, and alcoholic parties liberally sprinkled the place. The architecture (neo-Classical) of the Ball Room and Gambling House dominated this sinners' paradise. A wretched youth dangled by his neck from a window above the Loan Office in the Gambling House. Below it, mums pressed into the pawn shop, in much the same way as they did in our own streets. Near the end of the Broad Way, cavalry charged, cannons roared, and wounded horses fell on top of their riders. A train rushed over a bridge, with the words SUNDAY TRAIN printed on its white plume of smoke. The Sunday train impressed me deeply, both at this time and in later years when I forfeited a considerable fortune through travelling to the West Country on a Sunday excursion! And hell waited at the end of the Broad side of the picture. Black-winged demons floated about in it like a pantomime flying-ballet. In their clutches were the white forms of humans being flung to the flames of the burning city. Great scales hung through the smoke, weighing the souls of men and finding them wanting.

Savings Campaign

Perhaps more important than these inanimate symbols of sin were my own companions. They too must be exchanged for 'born again' friends, the profane sacrificed to the sacred. Setting up a home-made Inquisition, I decided on those I should shun, committing them to a mental *auto-da-fé*. Jack first, of course, He was a real sinner, and an insidious one, because he had caused me to be fond of him. He it was, after all, who led me into the 'valley of shadows', by taking me to séances. I contemplated his vanity for clothes, worship of music, weakness for food. His brittle mockery of what he termed hypocrisy but which to me had become faith, made me shudder. I might have become the same. What thanks I gave God that I was not as this other man.

Spies of my Holy Office investigated every former associate. Even little Mavis, we decided was not quite 'sound'. How could she be, wearing shorts to play badminton, and listening to Beethoven? Lingering doubts about the health of Mavis's faith, were dispelled at an evening together which proved to be our last. Sadie, her sister Phyllis, and I decided to go with Mavis to a concert. It was said not to be in any way 'worldly', and consisted of excerpts from the *Messiah*, to which nobody could object. It must have cost quite a bit to hire the big hall in the city centre. The choir looked impressively large. But when the female soloist sailed on to the platform I got a sharp dig in the ribs. Phyllis was shocked by the painted lips, but even more so by the full-length dress of red silk, naked of arm and shoulder—a real ball-dress! Now we must show our true colours, demonstrate our 'separation from the world'. In protest, observed by the whole audience, we got up and stormed out of the hall, leaving a bewildered Mavis behind. On the way out, however, I had to fight the Devil, who kept reminding me that this piece of witness had stung me for four shillings.

Phyllis usurped Mavis, and then, incredibly, Sadie herself. She was almost thirty, more than twice my age. By the time summer came we were taking tea together at the teashops kept by ladies in smocks. Though Latin-hued like her sister, Phyllis's voice fell so much softer on the ear, charming it by a Malone Road diction. This intimacy did not develop until I had joined Sadie's Tract Band.

Two such bands existed at the hall where I got 'saved', and the sisters belonged to one each. My membership entailed great honour. Usually people did not join until much later in life, and even then regarded it as a privilege. However, in spite of being the group's youngest member, I soon made a busy contribution. The big field-night was on Monday, though of course Band members carried a supply of tracts at all times, together with pocket Testaments. The Monday-nighters met at a given street-corner at a given time. Bundles of tracts were then handed round by the secretary. Loaded with ammunition, the snipers went into a corner, for a prayer-meeting. What must passers-by have thought of the suspicious gang in the black-out huddled together with bowed heads, the men hat-in-hand? Then we went in to attack, and spent a couple of hours pushing our tracts through letter-boxes. Yet another street-corner prayer-meeting followed the distribution. At the end of this caper, the younger ones—including Sadie and her boy-friend, went to a fish and chip saloon. If we had to queue, out came the tracts again, and naturally, we lost no opportunity of saying a loud grace over the chips.

On Thursdays we assembled again. And as though we had not prayed enough over our Monday tracts, we went to a complete fellowship. This was a great trial to me in the beginning because everyone present had to pray aloud and impromptu. We must pray direct from the heart—not with highfalutin phrases from 'unsaved' saints or from printed rituals. None would have dared to admit that in practice many of us used outworn, threadbare phrases in our appeals to the Throne of Grace. The more self-conscious among us went so far as to plan prayers beforehand. So much for spontaneity.

On my first Thursday I went unprepared to address the Lord in public (how much easier to shout righteous invective at sinners in the street) and consequently dried up. Nothing would come to my lips, except the Lord's Prayer. I considered *it* safe at least, and expected the others to join in. They remained silent, and one or two, I fancied, shot me disapproving glances. I had made a worse mistake than quoting Shakespeare. Opening my fingers to see whether the others were really horrified, I finished hurriedly.

Saying that prayer in public was no new experience. At about four years old I first did so in Sunday School; I opened my eyes then also. This was a sin I knew, for our teacher always reprimanded those who did. God must have whispered secretly, to inform her that our eyes were open during prayers. Obviously she would not open her own, I thought, because this too would constitute sin. Pointing a finger to her eye, she would give us silent reproach, and afterwards a lecture about not letting our minds stray from the solemn words we were saying. Easier said than done, missus. What did the words mean anyway? Some certainly had meanings, but concocted at that time from a childish theology of my own. At the start of the Sunday School when we went through the Lord's Prayer, my mind became a magic lantern showing me pictures at each new phrase, but they were not altogether the enjoyable slides they showed us on Wednesday nights at the children's service.

Once we were all standing up in Sunday School, a teacher

would begin in a monotonous voice, *Our Father*. Flash! A picture came in my mind of a very formidable old gentleman in a nightshirt, with two embroidered holes at the back to allow His wings to escape. *Which art in heaven*, another flash of the magic lantern, this time showing me a crystal river with silver spray dashing up, making the angels jump out of the way. Our most frequent hymn was 'Shall we gather at the river'. *Hallowed be thy Name*, now a slide appeared of the Holy Name *hallowed* (hollowed I thought it meant) in Gothic lettering, as on the texts in our parlour. But that did not satisfy us—the same ornate lettering must appear everywhere, over the pubs and pawn shops, triumphant on every stronghold of the Devil, if God was to rule the earth. *Thy Kingdom come*—great cloud-loads of descending heavenly bodies. *Thy will be done, in earth as it is in heaven*—making wills was a great pastime of our childhood, and of course, God's will was as vast as a roll of linoleum, tied round with all the seals we knew about from the Book of Revelation. *Give us this day our daily bread*—how I longed for the breadserver's horse to stop every day outside our house with fresh loaves, for in those days my mother could only afford old bread, called 'cuttin' loaves'. *Forgive us our trespasses, as we forgive them that trespass against us* —this one was easy and clearly referred to going on the railway lines, where a sign about trespassers stood. *And lead us not into temptation*—I galloped through this bit, as I had not the slightest intention of going the long way to school in order to resist the good things outside the greengrocer's. *But deliver us from evil*—may I always be able to run so fast that the black Devil with his intriguing horns and tail, will never catch up with me. *For thine is the kingdom*—a fantastic coronation set. *The power*—what steel-like muscles God must have to be capable of holding back the clouds and winds. *And the glory*—gold tassels and hospital whiteness everywhere. *For*

ever and ever—until next Sunday and the next night, until the
Sunday School prize-giving, and until the time when I am
so old that I must wear long trousers. *Amen*—a salute to God's
police who guarded heaven, just as our B-men guarded
Belfast.

However unsound my ideas may have been, at least I tried
to put meaning into my prayers as a child. But I found the
prayer-meetings of the Tract Band very painful, words came
with difficulty, and even then not always with meaning, and
the range of subjects was strictly limited. Friday's big session
was far superior. Before we began in the hall, one of the
elders emptied the prayer request-box, into which people had
slipped petitions for individual prayers. And we had the
missionary list to provide thrills. Our 'field' ranged from those
in the papish Free State to the 'poor black folk' in Africa, and
included the deaconess from our own circle now in Chili,
and the colporteur languishing in a German concentration
camp with his twin daughters. Original prayer could be
readily composed from such exciting themes. The main clue
to success lay in getting a chance early in the proceedings. I
would sit crossing my fingers nervously, trying to keep four
or five topics in mind, hoping fervently that those praying
before me would not mention them first, and so steal my
thunder.

For enjoyment, Wednesday nights topped the bill. We
held the Sunbeam Circle then, prior to mid-week fellowship.
When I was a child I had loved these breezy services enlivened
with rousing choruses and object lessons. But many pages in
the book of years had been turned since then. Now I was
fourteen and a leader, sitting at the end of a row trying to
keep the brats from shouting the place down with,

Savings Campaign

'A sunbeam, a sunbeam,
Jesus wants me for a sunbeam;
A sunbeam, a sunbeam—
I'll be a sunbeam for Him.'

My notebook soon filled up with sermons for children. I jotted them down mostly in acrostic form, meditations on such themes as L.O.V.E. or S.A.V.E.D. And to all the grown-up services I took pencil and paper to make notes of the texts and important points of the sermons. This good evangelical practice reached fever pitch at fellowship meetings. Only believers went to those, making the affair like a press conference with swiftly scribbling pens and pencils.

In holiness, no less than in other matters, practice makes perfect. Soon I learnt to 'lead' in prayer. That I could do this without embarrassment, and in convincing fluency, thanks were due to the influence of a very wild-fire evangelist indeed. He had come to give us a refresher course on the Epistle to the Romans. His extempore prayers always opened in an unexpected way, like new music, where excitement lies perhaps more in the opening bars than in development. This preacher plundered the Old Testament for highly-coloured and startling material. Of all his beginnings, none thrilled me more than, 'Not by the blood of goats and bullocks do we approach Thy throne . . .'.

This was talking sense, I thought, because it linked my new-found religion with my life's great love—farming. At Easter I went home to Fermanagh, determined to make good use of this splendid prayer-opening. The Methodists' winter Preachings still took place in local farmhouses. They had done so ever since John Wesley himself held kitchen services in the district. On the whole, Maggie felt pleased that I had been 'born again'. To her mind anything that would keep me away from Spiritualism, could only be good. But she would not be persuaded by my enthusiasm to land others in the evangelical net. My zeal almost drove us to quarrelling, especially when Maggie fetched her fiddle to set the dancers going. What I had once enjoyed, now seemed evil, so I sulked in a corner singing *Sacred Songs and Solos* at the top of my voice.

At Malhune's Preaching I really made a name for myself. Clambering over hedges and ditches, the country folk went to sit in the oil-lit kitchen and listen to the circuit minister. I knew all the farmers and their well-washed wives. Farm Preachings loomed large on the social horizon. They were always well attended. The minister at Malhune's turned out to be a friendly man. He opened the service, standing with his back to the open turf fire. He scanned the rows of creepies and settles, and those propped against the dresser. Was anyone present, he asked, who would like to 'lead' in prayer? But paroxysms of shyness seized the people, it seemed as if they had stopped breathing. Not an eyelash moved, and the crickets at the back of the hob, could quite plainly be heard singing. Then up I jumped and came out with my goats and bullocks.

It must have given everyone a shock. But they had time to recover, because I prayed a long time, and afterwards was invited up to the parlour to have supper with the minister. This honour even surprised Maggie. By next morning, the news of the public performance had spread far and wide into the countryside. When I wheeled the milk churns down for the creamery lorry, Joey Cartwright met me. 'That was a powerful prayer ya gave at the Preaching,' began this Free Stater who worked in the forest. He wanted to know all about the previous evening, but I felt much too grand to repeat it as requested, and told him to come the following night. I had already decided that we should have a Preaching at our own house, despite Maggie and Christy being strictly Church of Ireland.

They readily gave consent, however, and Maggie was so delighted to get out the big family Bible. We invited everyone we could think of, whether they would be likely to come or no. I sifted through my collection of assorted sermon notes and selected one with John 3 :16 as text. This particular sermon followed a familiar pattern of 'the greatest fact, the greatest act, and the greatest pact'. Delivered by me in my newly-acquired authoritative voice, it was bound to be a success. How deeply all this entered Maggie's soul could not be determined. Perhaps she regarded the whole thing as a rather elaborate charade. At any rate, just before the preaching was due to begin, she remembered her father's old frock-coat. It was a real preacher's garment, though now sadly green about the back. As an evacuee I had used this so often to christen the animals. But I had worn it inside-out, for the black silk lining and white sleeves possessed a more clerical appearance for me to carry the waters of baptism to the kittens and calves. Despite Maggie's disappointment I could not use the frock-coat now, for, of course, I knew of the evil attached to all dressing-up in order to preach the Word.

Surely, never had there been a Preaching like ours—and I was most certainly going to out-do Archdeacon Pratt, who was a prince of preachers. I sat in my bedroom off the kitchen waiting for the company. I kept an eye to the keyhole. To see Maggie's kitchen filling up was gratifying. Even more pleasing was to see that the men's caps were off—a custom never observed in the house except when offered food. My Preaching was being treated seriously.

What a pity it was, that Mrs. Malhune had refused to lend us her harmonium, though at least Sammy, their byreman, promised to come. In fact, I felt not at all encouraged to observe Sammy, through my vestry key-hole. Being a renowned and eloquent preacher himself round about, he promised to be my severest critic. But organ or no organ, Maggie tuned her fiddle, and we had enough hymn books to go round, shared one between two.

The service went beautifully, until half-way through the sermon. As I warmed to my subject (the lake of fire) and warned the farmers to abandon their evil lives (poor fellows, working from dawn till sunset, had little enough opportunity to sin) I noticed Maggie. She was holding her hands up to cover the grins that she could not control. At first, I thought I must be mistaken. Maggie laugh in a Preaching? Never. Passing on to words of salvation, I saw only too well that Maggie *was* laughing. In a moment of panic, I thought she was laughing at me. Then I followed the direction of her glances—old Sammy. He sat with his head nodding assent to my every word and kept up a continuous response of 'Amens' and 'Hallelujas'. They sounded especially loud when I paused for breath or thought. And then I wanted to laugh too. I finished quickly, not daring to look again at Maggie. She had infected me, for we always had disastrous results on each other so far as giggles were concerned.

Afterwards when the years had softened my fierce attitude about Preachings and the like, Maggie made a confession. She had, she admitted shyly, also been grinning at me. Maggie's face had never in her whole life been used to long periods of solemnity. How could she keep it straight when her ex-evacuee cub stood up in her kitchen, spouting such long words, 'predestination', 'procrastination' and the roof-raising 'omnipotency'—a word that always reduced her to a pulp from laughing.

Enthusiasm did not expire with the last breath on the last

line of the last hymn, at our kitchen service. Rather it increased. Although far from Sadie's Tract Band, I bravely carried on the work of the printed word. For miles around the countryside I rode my bike, pushing tracts into handles on milk churns at the head of lanes. A more enduring witness were the Gospel seals bearing texts. Designed for use on the backs of envelopes, the penny-sized sticky stamps could be used in all sorts of ways. I decorated my letters with them, of course, but the fun derived from finding more exciting places. The voice of doom-to-come could easily be stuck on top of obscenities scribbled over lavatory walls, or other seats of the scornful. By changing my place frequently, quite a rash of salvation could be left behind on buses and trains.

When a dance in the Orange hall was announced, I saw at once a golden opportunity of witness. Dancing itself was not permissible for me any longer. Not that I disliked dancing, but the 'saved' of earth could not indulge in it. *The Broad and Narrow Way* had early illustrated the condemnation hanging over ballrooms—from Isaiah 'And the harp, and the viol, the tabret, and pipe, and wine, are in their feasts: but they regard not the work of the Lord, neither consider the operation of his hands.' Well, consider they should, on this occasion at least. Though forbidden by conscience to set foot actually in the hall, at least I could go into the little cloakroom at the back. When the sinners came out after the dance for their coats, they would find Gospel tracts stuffed into their pockets. And I had just the right tract for dancers. What a potent effect the country boys and girls would suffer when they read it. Their minds were already in the mood to think of spiritual things. Most of them passed haunted lanes or houses on the way to and from the dance. What shocks my tracts must produce in their pronouncement that by next morning they might be dead!

Like a Father Christmas filling stockings, I went stealthily through each coat, depositing my tracts. But I also carried a supply of seals, and so I came outside. What delight I had from country dances of the past. We had always let down the tyres, and turned the saddles back to front on the girls' bicycles, or hid them altogether. When we 'helped' them in their distress later we could always count on a free roll in the heather. But this time the innocent had to suffer for the guilty. While I crept around the cycles, sticking my seals on them, three young Orangemen pounced on me. Set to guard the girls' bikes and remembering me from previous occasions, they presumed the worst. Struggling and protesting my good intentions, I was dragged to the bog-hole for a ducking. My righteous objections must have carried a note of conviction, for after screaming as loudly as I could, they let me go. Less than a year before they knew me as a wild evacuee who joined them swimming naked in the lake on the way home from Sunday church. Now I acted so grandly with my white collars and big Bible. Down in the bog, the three of them had hidden a bottle of drink, since alcohol was forbidden in the hall. To make amends for manhandling me, they offered me some. Drink! And me 'saved'! I snatched the bottle and flung it into the muddy waters of the bog-hole. Forgetting my grandeur, I was over the bog-bank and into our own plantation before they could catch me up and give me deserved punishment.

All of this afforded me immense satisfaction. There I was, alone, and in an almost hostile part of the world, carrying our banner. Not unlike a missionary really, I thought. My exploits pleased me so much that I wrote of them fully to Phyllis, perhaps more fully than the facts would justify. My account of events presented a Bayeux tapestry woven with scenes of my skirmishes and victories for the Lord. Sadie, alas, had now left the hardware and paint merchants to make final preparations for her wedding. Having earlier disposed both of Jack and Mavis, only Phyllis remained now as confidante. I wrote her reams, and ate my heart out waiting for replies. Even the scrappiest of her notes sent me into rhapsodies. Since Sadie was no longer packing up putty, I could see no reason for going back to Belfast and the shop, though Easter was over now. I certainly gave no week's notice, and as was becoming usual, got my mother to go along and fetch my insurance cards.

Now spring rushed over all the land in a flood-tide, breaking down the last resistance of winter, washing away November-nakedness in a wake of delicate green. When the sun peered out from the green-blue, sea-like sky, it struck hot on the skin. And clouds, driven from the Atlantic did not thunder across the sky in chariot-races, but drifted slowly by like powdered periwigs moving to inaudible minuets. I had never seen Maggie's farm so beautiful. For half a mile down the lane, daffodils frolicked in sensuous touches of air. Drifts of pale blossom piled on orchard boughs. By early May the sunny shores of the lake islands were baked hard, and gulls worked on old grass to furnish their fabulous nesting colony. The garden warbler returned with his mellow charms and a litter of hairy nests down in the bramble thickets of the old cow-pass. Fronds of fern and bracken held their spring races like fluffy caterpillars, to see which would be first in making the best bishop's crozier. My heart leapt with joy, and despite erotic dreams at night, by day salvation's glory filled me.

I passed my fifteenth birthday and started shaving.

We could not forget that last year's corn had been badly plundered by the rabbits on the hill. So we decided to do our quota of the accursed war-time, compulsory tillage down in the bog. We could always put a big potato crop to good use because Maggie had a mania for collecting St. Anthony's pet pigs. This decision involved hours of back-breaking work, for the seed had all to be sown in the traditional lazy-beds. We spread dung over the field straight on the grass, and pressed the seed potatoes into it. Then our long Fermanagh spades cut sods on three sides and folded them over to the fourth side, to cover up half of the ridge. We repeated this on the other half, so that the high ridge had natural drainage on eash side, and the hinged sods kept out the late frosts. To get into an easy rhythm of lazy-beds demanded great skill. Both sides of the hinged sods had to close as neatly as the finest triptych.

Pigeons went on with their muffled cooing in the bluebell woods as I sat under my favourite beech writing to Phyllis. Why did she still address me as 'Dear Brother in the Lord', when for four months now I had been her faithful watchdog? I was glad enough to hear from her about the Tract Bands, my special Sunbeams, and the Sunday services at the hall. But why, oh why, did not Phyllis send me one little acknowledgement of my daily overtures in the post? I felt like a watch-spring trying to drive Big Ben. The eternity I preached about, seemed to pass before a letter arrived, enclosing a photograph of Phyllis. I carried it about, ready for reference at any moment of the day. Undeniably slow though progress might be, it was faster by post than by our formal behaviour at the hall in Belfast. The most she ever allowed me to do was to carry her large Bible home, and maybe share an umbrella when it rained.

One day while I was out spreading turf in the bog, our grocer's daughter came tearing up the lane on her bicycle. Their shop also acted as post office and she brought a telegram for me. Trembling, I opened it. The head of the Tract Band, Sadie's new husband, asked me to return at once to Belfast, for he had got me a fine job. Taking the job meant immediate action, so reluctantly, I set off once again to the city next morning.

My relationships at home were worse than before. My mother could not afford to keep my room vacant just so that I could float in and out of the house whenever the fancy took me. Yet I resented the lodgers who dared to take down my *Broad and Narrow Way* to make way for shameless nude hussies from magazines. Not an hour passed after I got home before such a storm broke out that I took up my packed case and moved into lodgings. There was no hunting to be done for I knew exactly the place to go—a house run by 'good living' people. Before and after meals they said grace, and when visitors came, sang the 'Overcomer' grace. They did not dream like so many others, of Manx beaches and the lights of Blackpool, but only of the war ending and being able to go once again in the big tent at Keswick. The walls of all the rooms downstairs were covered with photographs of the famous convention speakers, mostly grouped in football rows round Bishop Taylor Smith.

Talking of such glories, the good people roused in me a longing to go and see the wonders of England for myself. But much more I felt drawn southwards, to countries of the sun where dwelt dusty millions of the 'unsaved' black folk. And the Lord, it seemed, was on my side. All things were working together for good. Even an initial setback I suffered, proved to be a disguised blessing. The job for which I came to Belfast, had already been taken. This did not depress me unduly, and my immediate reaction was to go for a few more weeks in Fermanagh. To my mother I appeared like a boat tacking aimlessly before any wind that happened to catch my sails. Jumping from job to job caused her to despair of my ever settling down to get a 'trade at my back'. Had I been living at home this latest zig-zag would undoubtedly have caused yet another row. Luckily she would never know.

Before I had time to take fresh bearings the miracle happened. Everyone plainly saw the hand of the Lord at work. My landlady's nephew was going as a missionary to West Africa. As though he were the first man about to be rocketed into astral space, relatives and friends rallied round him. A bumper send-off in the form of a valedictory service took place in a big hall down town. It was a believers-only affair, and they crowded the benches. The way some of the women ogled him made you think that savages' spears had already entered his well-covered body. Somebody spoke about his Society's 'field', and gave the farewell address. Then with emotion at its peak, a challenge was delivered. What other young souls sat now in the congregation who would follow him into 'the vineyard'?

A broadside delivered at such short range could hardly miss. The commanding question ran like liquid fire amongst us. These people got at you over this in the same way as when they determined to 'save' you. Only on this occasion, since all present were already 'born again', an outward sign different from the putting up of a hand would be necessary. Once again the rattle of trams filtered from the street. Over the bowed heads, the preacher beseeched the Holy Ghost to awaken the need of service in a believer's heart.

I peeped. The slit between my fingers revealed the young missionary on the platform. Lucky fellow. What a nice black suit he had on, and his hair so smoothly oiled. His big new tin travelling trunks must be packed by now. I had seen similar ones in Smithfield Market. Discarded after years of service, these still bore the arms of honour, half-scratched-off labels with fabulous tropical names. LAGOS, SAIGON, TOKYO, CALCUTTA. And the missionary's boat-ticket, that too must be ready, neatly printed with his name and cabin number, lying on his empty bedroom mantelpiece. No more worries for him. No more hardware and paint merchants, no more families to tie him down with apprenticeships and the getting of trades. Even his studies and awful examinations lay behind him. His horizons now were all blue sky. Conquests lay before him, the bringing of light to dark places, healing was in his wings. I saw the circle of black faces listening for the first time to well-loved stories of the Lord Jesus. I heard the echo of 'Abide with me' dying away among the palm-fringed clearing after Sunday evening service. Oh, that was life abundant for you!

Almost involuntarily, I started from my seat, and stood up, quivering with excitement. My movement released the tension. And as my day-dream faded, as the South Sea surf receded, and Gauguin's golden bodies (decently clothed, of course) vanished again, a shower of 'Amens' fell on me from the good people of the hall. I had received the 'Call' and from henceforth was a separated person—a missionary in embryo.

In a twinkling of an eye, one of my life's oldest and most cherished ambitions was realized—practically. A rush of childhood memories crowded in on me. The scores and scores of missionaries I had heard preach, the hundreds of magic-lantern pictures I had watched spellbound from the age of five, all these experiences were to be mine in reality!

One or two tedious problems needed surmounting, my age for instance. I had grown over six feet tall by now and looked at least like a young man of twenty. When the missionary society heard that, in fact, I was only just fifteen, their enthusiasm noticeably waned. The hall people who knew me, backed me up, said what a 'grand testimony' I had, and made laudable comments on my 'keenness'. Something had obviously to be done, so the evangelist who conducted the valedictory service invited me to his house for tea. Since I was out of work and fond of farming, he wondered if I would like to stay with friends of his in County Antrim. This stone would kill all sorts of birds because his friend also ran a country mission hall, and was for ever starved of speakers. I could take over for a few months and get really established in the faith. Though I might be in the teens of my physical powers, in the spiritual life I was yet a suckling. And so on, until I saw sense and recognized the value of local witness until I reached an age for missionary training. In no time at all, it seemed, the whole thing was fixed up.

How proud I felt, to be stopped in the street by the staunchest of elders and greeted with, 'I heard you've got "the Call",' as though I had just had a baby.

CHAPTER IX

Loving Shepherd

Apaling topped by many strands of barbed-wire, separated our entry at home from the lush railway verges. Old sleepers had been stood on end to make this high fence. And between the thick baulks of wood the mare's-tails grew, like miniature pine trees in a steep valley. With the shaggy mare's-tails are associated my first love and sexual experience. I was about five years old.

We had nailed the old tarpaulin, that usually covered the mangle, to the fence, making ourselves a fine tent. The narrow slits in the paling lit the tent with shafts of light, like lancet windows in a cathedral nave, or Norman slots for shooting arrows through. Invariably we played hospitals in there, dressing and undressing, and lying flat on the entry cobbles as though on a ward bed. Over our heads, the sun baked the thick canvas, and the black earth between the small round stones, smelt of cat and dog. But I remember the tingling, rousing sensation of mare's-tail best of all. An older girl assumed the role of matron and I lay at her feet. I cannot recall whether the punkah-fanning of my body with the mare's-tail formed part of the cure for my pretended illness. But I well remember the sensation induced by the light green tresses which stimulated my every tissue to erotic excitement.

We had only started the second book at school when I assumed the part of doctor, and consequently explored others' bodies with these green magic wands. By my tenth year I fell seriously in love. My passion unleashed itself on one of our school's younger teachers who taught my sister. Heaven had given her Miss Greyfell as a name. Delightfully silky, curly coils of hair clung about her ears like grapes on a sun-drenched wall. The first time I ever saw the Mona Lisa's smile, the hovering look about Miss Greyfell's lips came to mind. When I began to find pleasure in thinking of her, I imagined Miss Greyfell with the buns of hair let down and walking about her room with nothing on. After all, it was only a short step from the entry 'hospital' examinations as children to a more grown-up version of the same thing.

Because I was an orphan, sweet Miss Greyfell always treated me with special kindness. Also because I had no father I knew well enough where she lived. The church orphan fund provided me with a pin-hole card to have punched when I collected money. Many were the pin-holes pierced by my Miss Greyfell. Falling for her came easier to me than falling off a log. One day I waited in her hallway, while she went to get some coppers and a pin to pierce my card. Quickly, almost without knowing what I was doing, I pulled her coat towards me, and buried my nose in its folds. Its mingled scents, all redolent of her, swept me into a rush of sensuality. The smells, of powder and scent, and a faint, lingering body-odour seemed the distillation of everything I ever dreamt about her.

I dreamt about Miss Greyfell a lot. So much, that one summer day when I called with my card and found her house empty, I broke in. My immediate thought was of the coat in the hall. It might still be there. Getting in the house presented no problem. I ran my penknife blade along the slit in the pantry window. A quick leap and the prospector was ready to strike the hidden gold veins of Miss Greyfell's intimate life. The wealth of ore around him, confused the miner, and he felt fearful of discovery. In fact, I stayed only long enough to drag her hairbrush over my face and legs (I still wore short trousers then) and take the remains of some cold pie. But next day I returned, and the next. The days grew into a whole summer month, and each time I became bolder. The discovery of Miss Greyfell's bedroom crowned my exploration. It surprised me to find the bed unmade. Nothing in the house seemed so closely linked with her as this. Her living, breathing, love-effusing body spent many hours in it. The bedclothes enveloped her like a wave folding on the shore. It would be impossible to find a way of being nearer to her. Without hesitation, I stripped off and jumped in. The sheets struck cold on my skin as though I had dived into a lake. To see what greeted Miss Greyfell when she first woke in the mornings, I closed my eyes and opened them. What a number of pillows she had. Under one I found a little bag of sweets.

A 'visit' early in the second month proved to be the last. I was caught red-handed. A key clicked in the front door lock, and I just had time to flee into the kitchen and hide behind the gas cooker. My heart punched so hard and rapidly that I thought I would die. Steps came straight for the kitchen, and the door swung back violently. Miss Greyfell screamed when she saw my humped-up body, and the un-hideable long legs sticking out beside the cooker. She ran into the hall, but I was after her, imploring her not to call the police. She wept, I wept. And such harrowing pictures did I draw of what would happen to me if I ran away from Belfast, which I would do if she called the police, that she let me run off home. Her goodwill almost came to nothing. Burglars had already been in the district and Miss Greyfell's house already reported to the police. The whole story came out, and my mother left my legs quite blue after a beating. But the Sisyphean efforts of our Rector were needed on my behalf, to save me once again from the remand home.

The course of true love ran on. Though only eleven, romantic high-tragedy tasted too sweet for me to abandon it. Police prosecution did not cure me of Miss Greyfell—ever. Her type became my ideal. Though the delicate strands of love that tied me to her, were harshly severed, ever afterwards I sought to bind them again to similar souls embodied in similar sweet flesh. Some fragrance of her clung about my hapless love for Sadie, and even more about the older Phyllis. Yet none charmed with the same voice that lilted like a running brook. Nor had any of them the fine, light skin, softer-drawn than the softest silk of a Chinese empress. Sadly, I reflected often, that in all the years ahead, I would never meet Miss Greyfell's like.

There was no need to have been so depressed.

My surmise turned out to be wrong, blissfully wrong. The moment I set my suitcase down at the Stramford's farm and Gertie shook my hand, I knew I had been wrong. Gertie kept house for her farmer brother Leslie, and their old uncle. My arrival upset her slightly, as I had come earlier than expected, and found her unprepared. Her hair was still put up in four plaits, dangling round her neck like four bell-ropes in a belfry. Two other little plaits, turned with paper, lay on top like wilting horns. But nothing could escape my eye. I saw that she brushed her hair into burnished gold-leaf tresses of the kind so common among the gipsies. With an artist's vision I knew it would ripple gloriously about her head like Miss Greyfell's when she dressed for the afternoon. In less than a glance I took all this in, from top to toes that looked neat enough in the big, soft leather boots, buttoned like skating boots. Her neck intrigued me most. It rose, a delicate pillar, swelling in a slight Modigliani-like entasis. Perhaps a slight touch of goitre lent it this fullness. I thought instinctively, how wonderful it would be to touch.

My heart leapt as Gertie led me into a spacious reception room. In a voice that was exactly Miss Greyfell's, she explained the domestic arrangements. Because I had come chiefly to conduct services at the hall, they had given me their best parlour to use as a study. A bed had been placed in one corner. Clearly the Stramfords had not the slightest idea of my age. Pleased, but not without some feelings of awe, I unpacked. When my notebooks, and Bible, and Cruden's *Concordance* lay scattered about the table, I went into the large farm kitchen. There I met Uncle. He was nearly ninety, but still a great worker on the farm, and about the nearest thing to an Old Testament prophet I had ever seen. Uncle sat on a long horse-hair sofa, generally referred to as 'the pitch'. Immediately following dinner he took his siesta on the pitch. Majestic spectacle! The white beard glistened in a ray of sun that got by geraniums in the window. The brown leathery features relaxed, and hands clasped each other over the patriarchal stomach, as though guarding the numerous tiny medallions that swung from the twin festoons of gold watch-chain. No marble knight or bishop recumbent on a tomb ever filled cathedral aisles with such calm dignity as Uncle on the pitch. Such tombs with their lions and cushions reminded me of Uncle and the horse-hair roly-polys that supported his hoary head and holey socks.

Leslie, the farmer, came in to dinner. An immense shyness governed his behaviour and I took to him immediately. Goodness knows what the Belfast evangelist wrote to him about me, but while I was there Leslie left the saying of grace to me, despite his position as head of the house. A young man took a place at the end of the table. No one seemed to include him in any conversation, except Gertie, who could not be too sure that he ate enough. Leslie introduced him as his nephew Tim. Not until Uncle unfastened his butterfly collar and settled on the pitch, did I venture to ask Gertie if Tim was another sister's son. I knew that Gertie was Miss Stramford. But no, she said, Tim wasn't. Whose then, I asked. Very coyly, and with a half-sunlit, half-shadowed smile, Gertie pointed a finger at her own breast.

Thumping with all its might, as though behind the gas cooker again, my heart threw me into confusion, as Gertie and I faced each other. She, a 'saved' woman, the mother of a 'wee love bird'? Surely, this must be, ought to be, impossible. Such a thing could not even be considered. But it *had* been possible, apparently, though probably not considered. And though Tim might be a muted harmony in her life, Gertie took an obvious pride in him. For this, and for her frankness and lack of hypocrisy about the affair, I thought her wonderful. What sky could hold a brighter star than mine now did?

Two free days would elapse before my first preaching engagement. As agreed before leaving Belfast, I set about helping Leslie with the work out-of-doors. None of the other farms I had ever lived on kept sheep. And now I discovered fresh delights in being taught shepherding. Symbolism of my future as a missionary imprinted every move we made across the hill, and even the words we used. Clipping and dipping were over, so the main job was to round up the flock on the hill, and with an expert eye, look for maggots. An unusually active tail warned us of this menace in a sheep's body. Aided by the dogs we drove our sheep down to the farm and dipped any infected parts. The prolonged hot summer days turned the sheep-cotes into ovens, for they were only roofed with galvanized iron. Laboured breathing by the sheep filled the sheds like the sound of plaguing locusts.

Within a week I could go out confidently to the hill and round up the flock on my own. I loved this. Vast silence canopied the hills, enhanced by peewits that started up from the grass, piping protests at the panting dogs. As I climbed, the world below diminished, houses, trees, cows, the ribbon of road all shrunk as though I had swallowed bottlefuls of 'Drink me' from *Alice in Wonderland*. Then at last came delicious isolation. Up there, climbing, sweating, reaching for the sweeping hill-brow, I was free, free of all hull and gantry skylines, free of dark paint shops, free even of musty mission halls where, somehow, my life had led me. True I could see the country hall in the glen below. In the sparkling sunlight it shone virgin white against the charcoal shaded mountains. But it seemed different from drab city halls. Every breeze that caught my burning cheeks and forehead, came heavy with heather scent. And I knew the moor fragrance blew in the little hall's windows, where stray dusty bees knocked helplessly to escape. No noisy trams would shatter the sermon's dramatic pause, down there. Nothing harsher than coughing sheep or mice scurrying in the wainscotting would harm the deep night-hush.

Once reached, the hilltop gave on to a wide moor, and a panorama of limitless sky. I could see across the Channel and to the purple Scottish coast beyond. Here, the sense of loneliness intensified, even the flitting wheatears ignored me, and darted erratically about their business. Swamps joined each other in a long chain over the moors, deep enough in places to be tiny lakes. A small bridge spanned one narrow sheet, its rotting wood lacquered in green slime. By warning me never to cross this bridge, Gertie revealed much about herself. I had no fear of falling in, for I could swim. But water terrified Gertie, as it did the whole family. Fine beaches lay within easy cycling distance of the farm, and although the summer

heat went on relentlessly day after day, I could never get any
of the family to go with me. This hydrophobia dated from
many years before when a young brother drowned. Gertie's
parents had been shore-dwellers, adding to a meagre livelihood by kelp burning farther along the coast. But when
Kenneth drowned they forsook the sea, giving up their
wrack rights, and moved over to Uncle's two-parloured
farm. Since then Gertie had never put her whole body in
water, not even in a hip-bath.

And this, in a way, stirred up the old trouble. Quite un-
wilfully, visions of Gertie bathing in a hand-basin, began to
devour me.

They never sent milk to the creamery, although the farm
was twice the size of Maggie's in Fermanagh, and kept as
many milk cows. Instead, Gertie churned it all. I did not hold
with women having to do all the milking, and so night and
morning I helped her. Neither could I see sense in the old
tradition they honoured, whereby men used the stable for a
lavatory, while the women used the byre. For me it seemed
far superior to squat amongst the bog-cotton with sun, moon
or stars for company and contemplation.

Gertie and I carried the buckets of milk into the dairy and
poured it through the separator. Except for the tumble-
churn, this large red machine was the dairy's only concession
to modern times. Shallow, stave-built tubs stood around, and
huge butts for buttermilk. Most of the utensils Gertie used
in dressing the butter, were solid turnery, bowls, ladles, and
the most ornate butter stamps, all made of wood. Nobody
had used the old horse-churn for some years now. The
tumble-churn's rumblings and splashings never failed to
warn me that Gertie had started in the dairy, whenever I was
about the house. No matter what I might be doing, she liked
me to go and 'swing my bacon', for luck lay in giving the

handle a few turns. I was quick to see with what eagerness
Gertie awaited my visits to the dairy. Punctually at nine
o'clock on Saturday mornings, Leslie led the mare and best
trap to the half-door, and we loaded it with the baskets of
butter. Dressed in his best leather leggings and high-domed
bowler hat, Uncle got in and drove off to town six miles
away.

I had constantly to keep in mind, however, that the farming I loved so much was not the main reason for my being
there. When I watched the lazy, grateful cows turning out of
the byre, or saw the sheep dotting the hillsides as their wool
dotted the fences that caught it, a pang would strike me.
Even on the lark-riven hill, I knew this wholly-golden life
could never be mine. High purposes leading to life eternal,
drew me away from the things of earth, even such a beautiful
earth as I found in County Antrim. To a plough of sorts, I
had indeed put my hand. From it there could be no looking
back. The parlour window attracted me more than the parlour table. On the one lay my sermon notes and hymn lists.
But the other gave me a view of thorn-shaded meadows and
leafy woods where I longed to lie. I never doubted that the
Lord had given me 'the Call', but at times what had sounded
initially as a trumpet note became no more than a squeak.
The Epistles to the Thessalonians could be tiresome when the
shorthorns were lowing at the gate.

Services in the mission hall never failed to revive the red-
hot gospeller in me. An audience dispelled faint faith merely
by the opening notes of a hymn. The mid-week fellowship
had been my first engagement at the hall. By way of introducing myself, I gave my 'testimony', a post-mortem on how
I became 'saved'. Twenty or so people attended. Most of
them seemed to be related either to the blacksmith or his
brother, the postman. Within a month I had been invited to

every farm, and given tea in the parlour as though I were already a missionary. It did not need much ferreting to discover that Gertie was not on good terms with the blacksmith's daughter, who was younger. This daughter figured as a power in the community, and I frequently called on her to give the opening prayer. She enjoyed this despite having a bad lisp. Gertie on the other hand would have been mortified to say anything out loud in public. Even an ordinary 'Amen' could not be managed. But as soon as the doxology had been sung at the end of the meeting, and hand-shaking started, Gertie's voice rose above all others.

Teasing had long been a favourite sport of mine, so now I began threatening Gertie that at the next meeting I would call on her to lead the prayer. Horror filled her eyes as she pleaded to be left in peace. When I refused to relent, Gertie said very well, she would not go to the hall at all. But I knew otherwise, for she had no other outing in the whole week. Finally departed I could reduce her to tears by casually bidding her not to make too long a prayer. She never really trusted me, that I would not suddenly pounce on her in front of everybody.

To keep Gertie busy, a daily baking of bread took place in the kitchen. A deep meal-ark contained the sack of flour at one end, and it stood near the fire to prevent dampness. And I sat on the ark one day drying myself after a heavy shower had caught me unawares as I weeded turnips. Along came Gertie to get her flour for baking, from the ark. 'Why, you're steaming,' she said accusingly. Concern filled her voice when she demanded that I change clothes at once. Our friendliness had developed to the point now where we could take liberties in what we said. Instead of moving off the ark, I spent the next ten minutes arguing about colds that did or did not lead to pneumonia. At first I presumed that her extraordinary concern for me stemmed from my having 'the Call'. Gertie felt no qualms of doubt that her brother and son still out in the rain, would keep sound chests.

As we argued, and her worry for me grew more evident, I began to wonder if it originated in some emotion other than respect for my exalted status as missionary candidate. Tim told me that until I arrived at the farm, Gertie had never been so dressed-up during the day. Now, as we bickered in the kitchen, the truth flashed on me. Gertie and me! My body tingled expectantly as though captive again under the mare's-tail stethoscope. At last, Gertie resorted to tears, pretended ones. When she came over to the open meal-ark, I refused to budge. During the slight struggle that followed, I planted a kiss on the neck, right on the centre of the fleshy little ruff that made the whole head so unique. I dashed into the yard, before she could lift her wooden beetle against me.

Elated, but anxious, I waited the call to go in for dinner. When the hand-bell rang out as usual, I held back. Leslie and Tim came to the yard with old sacks as towels and washed their hands in the stone trough. I joined them and together we went in to eat. Uncle was already supping busily away at his plate while we waited behind our chairs. Not being a 'Christian', Uncle had no cause to wait for grace. But he courteously laid his knife and fork down while Gertie stood at her place. I caught her eye as she indicated that I should say the grace. The clatter of steel on china ensued. Curls of steam wound up from the potatoes as though incense to our 'For these and all Thy mercies Lord. . . .' No restraint could be sensed in our chatter. But guilt for the kiss weighed me down, and I could not bear to look at Gertie. When Uncle had given a good belch and settled down to the pitch, I went out for my own forty winks in the hayshed.

Gertie's dinner and the hayshed's close heat defeated me. I

fell asleep at once, but to wake with a start. While hunting out the hen's nests in the hay, Gertie saw my shoeless feet and could not resist tickling them. Her eyes, white in the dim shed, were all mischief. In a flash I had her down on the hay. She fought hard as I tried to get off the skating boots, and pleaded about the eggs our threshing bodies must surely be crushing. When I began to tickle, she screamed hysterically and threw me off with the power of a man. Her strength surprised me, perhaps because it was such delicate skin that concealed her muscles. Over and over we rolled, getting hotter and hotter, until the struggle ended. For a moment we lay spent, our arms still entwined in readiness for another attack. We did not slide our arms away.

I was young and lusty, and it was summer. And so I knew my first love.

Darkness and shame drowned me as passion ebbed away. Without a word to Gertie, who lay calm and breathing lightly, I jumped up and ran out of the stifling hayshed. Looking at nothing, I ran heedlessly. All hell must be jeering me now, I thought, for this defiling of my body, the temple of the Holy Ghost. Over the fuchsia ditch, stumbling in the rabbit burrows of the bracken pastures, on through the stirk grazing, then towards the hill I ran, neither halting nor looking back, until well away from the farm, and only the wethers knew I moved on the moor. Serenely, early afternoon baked the upland. The distant sea went mauve, its horizon gauzy with heat.

By the swamps I saw the rotten bridge. I flung myself on the ground and prayed. Was it really sin . . . was I now a 'backslider'? It was imperative to know. With bitter introspection I surveyed my life. Even from my earliest years I saw plainly how I had been a lustful person. At the infants' school, only the boldest girls would sit beside me. And even in those innocent days, on hearing the story of Potiphar's wife, I had thought Joseph a jinny for not getting out of his troubles the easy way. For years wonder at my own body filled many odd moments. I marvelled at the numerous ways it reacted to touch or heat, smell or sound. Without my telling it, my body would do things of its own accord. What thrills I enjoyed because my nose picked up a waft of Miss Greyfell's perfume in the school corridor. And Wagner had not been the only one to finger silk for inspiration. My 'conversion' at the Belfast hall had meant a daily fight against 'the world and the flesh'. But now they had sprung out and utterly destroyed me.

Gertie on the other hand, had relaxed into the hay again, when we released each other. She behaved quite naturally and seemed to suffer no distress about 'backsliding'. Gertie was a good woman and 'saved', maybe the sin. . . . But no clear answer would come, and so I presented my case to God. If I had committed a great sin, He must deal plainly with me. 'Conversion' did not take away a habit indulged over the years. By it, I confronted the Almighty with certain propositions by which he had to prove Himself. And an idea occurred to me now. I would close my eyes and walk over the treacherous, rotten bridge. If God wanted to show me the evil of my ways, the thing would collapse under me—and should I fail to drown, then I would fling myself over the cliff instead. I hurried to the bridge and set foot on it. Slowly, step succeeded step. Advancing deliberately, I prayed aloud for God to judge me. Cold sweat streamed down from my forehead, smarting in my eyes. Hay-seeds inside my shirt set up a frightful itching.

By good luck the bridge held. It swayed, but not one of its slats gave way. Not a little shaken I reached the other side. Now I sweated with relief. Apparently He had decided to give me another chance. God got a humble prayer of thanks for that. Then the shutters of my soul went up, so that He could not peer in and announce a change of His mind. Behind the shutters, I relaxed, much as a prisoner who gets a reprieve must do.

A track wound down to the sea, and I ran again, this time shouting for joy, and frightening one or two lazy ewes out of the way. High waves surged into a little cove, spilling a fleecy train of foam up the sand. Where the water scooped itself up before thundering over and racing inshore, I dived. Powerful currents inside the breaking waves turned me in underwater somersaults. The sand-wash and pebbles scraped against me, until at last, popping out like a sausage from a machine, I was chucked out by the wave to sprawl in the sucking shallows. Deep refreshment entered the body that so lately had snared the soul. I could not help the exuberance that the cold water and warming sun gave me. The sea had made me *clean*. Tired and hungry I returned to the farm. Gertie dashed out to me, but said nothing of the hayshed affair. Her 'worldly' cousins had come on a visit, and Gertie did not want to serve tea until I changed into my good suit and said grace.

That night I had already gone to bed downstairs in the parlour, when Gertie's steps sounded across the yard. The cats were getting their supper served in the barn. Her soft voice calling the cats, scattered the hundred promises and pledges I had made since crossing the bridge. Like a shot, I pulled on my shirt and corduroys and was beside her. Within a week no guilt remained, though the pleasure grew greater. Blissful peace invaded the farm and all our lives now. We went into the fields and won a fine harvest. Uncle maintained his position as the best thatcher despite his age and worked on top of the hay pikes even in the strongest winds which came inland

from the sea. Using the ruck-shifter, I brought corn home
from the far hill. After each load Gertie came to the kitchen
window to wave me off. The fire in my blood now had sweet,
rewarding things to consume. Rebellion against my family
and hatred of Harry vanished like the hayfield's morning
dampness. My bliss came from the tranquil passing of time,
measured not by minutes but by simple incidents. On going
into the kitchen I might find Gertie ironing my shirt, or we
might steal a daring kiss in the kitchen while Uncle slept.
Arm in arm Gertie and I walked through the moon-scalloped
hedgerows to the fellowship hour. Occasionally we cycled
together over to her married brother's farm for tea, and we
always stopped at the cove to hurl pebbles into the sea. And
though late autumn came and caught us unawares by its hot
days, I still swam. Poor Gertie would stand petrified, praying
until I emerged from the waves, flushed pink for her to dry
my back.

Our delectable harmony was made poignant by infrequent
dissonances. These took the form of quarrels over my ration
book. War-time food restrictions brought no change to most
farms and Gertie's was no exception. We had more than
enough butter and Gertie made delicious cheese. A lot of fowl
came and went from our table, and from his solitary wandering with a gun on the moor, Tim often brought back something tasty for the pot. Uncle sparked off the ration book
arguments. Being a stickler for observance of law and order
he demanded my coupons to put with the others in his
leather wallet. This went off with him on Saturday morning
for the collection of the week's groceries from town.

However sternly Uncle might demand my book, I could
never surrender it. A powerful reason that I could not divulge,
prevented me. Gertie and Uncle must have thought it extremely odd the way I shied like an unbroken colt each time

the subject came up. I did not want Gertie to see that my ration book was a blue child's one. Questions of age had already risen, for Gertie's own puzzled me. 'Forty if a day' I teased her. But she said I was very wide of the mark. I tried to work it out from Tim's age, but never could. On the other hand, Gertie longed to know mine. 'Twenty?' she would ask coaxingly. But I laughed and said if she would first tell me hers, I would do likewise. And this I knew she never would.

But Uncle was a tiresome old devil and insisted on my ration book. It upset Gertie terribly to see him bang his blackthorn stick across the table. What shame he brought on the house too, doing this in front of me—I who had 'the Call' and who filled the mission hall with such numbers from far and near—some even whispered of 'revival'! But not having respect for my cloth, as it were, Uncle continued to bang the blackthorn until a day excursion into the town became inevitable. I got my blue ration book from its hiding place in the bottom of my case. It could be exchanged for emergency coupons in the town. These had no dreaded blue colour to betray me, so my age would remain a secret. The town had no attraction for me and I left for the farm immediately I got the cards. Uncle wanted to know how I had fared. The yellow emergency tickets did not please him. He turned them over in his hands suspiciously as though they were forgeries. Only the first visit to the grocer's convinced him of their soundness.

Leslie's attitude was different. He could not do enough for me, and encouraged me in both my lives, pastoral and spiritual. The high regard Leslie held for a widow was even confided in me. She had only come recently to the valley with her delicate son, to start a chicken farm. Harmonium-playing ranked among her accomplishments, so she played in the services at our hall. Deviously, so as not to cause alarm,

Leslie soon discovered her favourite hymn. But he could not screw up enough courage to invite her to supper after the fellowship. Next spring promised to aid Leslie, not only with its throb of rising sap, but also because the widow wanted him to go over and do their ploughing.

Tim remained mysterious and aloof. Although I tried hard to be friends, he always withdrew to an inner brooding, when my advances threatened his independence. The barrier may have between us because he was 'unsaved', and somehow felt himself left out of things. But Tim would not respond to Gertie's pleading that he should come to the hall while I was there. Not a fraction of his precious liberty would be surrendered. Uncle did not approve of his great-nephew, and Tim cared nothing for him. On most mornings, he chose to lie in bed until late, and he always avoided as much of the farm work as possible. Gertie could not bear to chide him, and while he was in the house nobody else would dare to do so, not even Uncle, for all his table-whacking with the blackthorn. Nobody knew exactly how Tim spent his time. When not up on the moors snaring or shooting, he would cycle off to some secret rendezvous. Seldom would he sit down at the table with us except for dinner, and when he did, those black eyes did not wander far from his plate.

Something sad and noble clung about Tim, and only Gertie could divine his far-away thoughts. Seen in retrospect, theirs was a beautiful relationship, and with the 'saved' business forgotten, a holy one. When they sat together in a room, they filled it with tranquillity. Tim stooped worse than I did. Old gossips said that round-shouldered illegitimates got their humps from being hidden in turf-creels among the hay when babies. Had Gertie hidden Tim in this way from the domineering Uncle? But I would never ask. Our love had no room for idle gossip. We would rather choose hymns for the next meeting, as we walked together through the autumnal valley, than cloud our minds with 'worldly' things. And both our consciences now accepted our relationship and all it involved, for were we not both 'born again Christians'?

Neither of us knew whether the others in the house were aware of our love. But they could hardly have missed the symptoms. Gertie and I constantly sought each other's company. When other people were present, and physical contact of touching hands or exchanged kisses, was impossible, then we fondled with our eyes. Tim may well have sensed the bond between his mother and me, and resented it. If that was so, it did not show in any violent form. Perhaps the misty depths of his eyes held more sadness than usual—a sadness that he could have scarcely explained. Gertie felt quite certain, however, that Uncle remained oblivious of our mutual love. He spent all his time working, eating and sleeping, and took little notice of the human scene around him. Or so we thought, for it was Uncle who tolled the knell of my passing day.

October had come and gone. Summer ended in a blaze of Byzantine glory, the dome of heaven lavishly covered with the gold mosaic of autumn leaves. Gold was everywhere, in light falling on the white chapel, in the valley woods, on mountain ridges when they caught the sun's last rays. Then the potato lifting was over for another year, and the lamb sales were done. Full of summer fatness, the rams were set out to find their ewe-harems up on the moor. And at last, gales swept the valley, stripping the trees and moaning among the black boughs. The high winds thundered about the housetop making the bright kitchen seem more homely and secure than before. Three months had been the length of stay originally planned for me. They were up now, but I made no attempt to move.

Then one Saturday, Uncle returned from town in a bad humour, and gave the first indication that the idyll was at an end. He could not bear to be dependent on anybody and carried it to absurd lengths. If anything was missing Uncle would never ask, but hunted for it himself. On that Saturday, he came in wet from the rain, but could not find the towel. He trundled about the kitchen like a badger in a hedge. Rumbles of annoyance warned me of trouble. I had not the wit to think what he wanted, and certainly had no idea that I was sitting on the towel, until he pulled it roughly through the back of the chair. But Uncle was in no mood for my apologies. All he wanted was a direct answer to his direct question as to when I proposed leaving. Remembering the ration book, I knew Uncle meant what he said. Nothing could be done. Gertie did not say much, but I could read sorrow in her soft eyes.

A big pair of ram's horns was kept on the parlour table. Somebody had made them into a pen-rack with inkwells in the base. The ram responsible for the ugly volutes had won several prizes, and I had often admired the horns' suggestion of strength. When Gertie presented the thing to me as a parting gift, astonishment almost choked my thanks. Dear Gertie, she could not bear to think of all the future sermons written by those pens out of those inkwells and preached by me that she would not hear. But I faithfully promised to cherish her gift and always to pray for her when using it. When in my African mission compound, the ram's horns on my bamboo desk would bring back again the green glens and the face of someone who loved me. Much more sensibly, the country congregation presented me with an umbrella, an essential part of a preacher's attire. I promised that it too would go to Africa—for use in the rainy season.

Since no bus passed the farm, Gertie took me in the horse

and trap to a stop on the coast road. Winter had come now to that favourite cove. The bus would not arrive for some time, but Gertie did not wait, as the girls up the valley might see her. Cracking her whip, she put the big brown mare into a gallop. A curve in the road hid her and we could wave no more.

The sea, folding over the broken shore, seemed to hold back something of my wonderful fifteenth summer,

So summer lingers—
long shadow fingers
clutching still, though snow
lies where lovers go
joined, as twilight
touches day and night.
Summer (shade or sun,
banks where minnows run,
exfoliated trees,
out-of-nowhere breeze,
brass-bold rocks,
the esoteric pool which locks
antediluvian lore
along the tide-tidied shore)
lovers true or fickle
feel no cruel winter sickle.
In landscapes stripped bone-stark
Love sings louder than the once-loud lark.

CHAPTER X

Second Blessing

Nothing that happened to me now could obscure my bright vision of the sun-countries. Only time needed to pass, and then I would be there. My jungle house in the mission clearing had long received its architectural form in my mind. The house consisted principally of a palm-leaf roof and a wide verandah. Here the sick 'black folk' would queue up for their red medicine and sticking-plaster by day. Later the verandah would be my night-parlour for listening to the stirring forest. Why the authorities wanted me to hang about in Belfast, I could not understand. Two years must go by before I could even start 'training', whatever that meant. The mission people did not seem at all impressed because I could plough, reap, sow and mow, nor that I could vet animals, handle a carpenter's bench, could even tailor and bake, cut hair and lay bricks. I knew my Bible and was recognized as an efficient 'soul-winner'. What more did the vineyard tiller need?

Elders maintained that little could be done until my eighteenth birthday. But a hard kernel of conviction in me insisted that a start on the road to Africa could be made when the important sixteenth birthday came in April. Mine was no pie-in-the-sky attitude to the whole thing, but down-to-earth and practical. Money, of course, would be needed to further my plans, or what, inspired by the mission hall, I called 'the Lord's plan' for me. Even the 'black folk' who looked after my piglets would need beads and trinkets as payment, and such things could not be got without money. (A film of Stanley finding Livingstone, seen in my 'worldly' days, still constituted my chief idea of Africa.) The hundred pounds I had set myself to acquire while an evacuee, had now been doubled, and I was still adding to it. Throughout the summer Gertie gave me hoards of butter and eggs, which I promptly sold at best black-market prices to the eager evangelicals of the city. Profits accrued in a very satisfactory way.

But now the hard Belfast pavements were under me, and I was again jobless. Weary calls at labour exchanges and newspaper offices began once more. However, life with Gertie had given me the sweet taste of being important (we had the silver teapot every day—not just on Sundays). So now I was not to be fobbed off with the fifteen shillings a week, that most lads of my age were offered. At one interview, if I would become his apprentice, a tailor offered me five shillings a week. Though love seeketh not its own, nevertheless I decided to use the network of influence with which evangelicals in high places covered the city. Quite a few of them had heard of the fiery young preacher. A discreet word there, a hint here, a suggestion dropped at the prayer-meeting, could work wonders. And it did, for a chemist took me in and awarded me a disproportionately large wage which could be supplemented by fire-watching. This pleased me, because a missionary should know something about medicines, and there could be no better place to learn it than behind a chemist's counter.

Summer with Gertie had settled me. A lot of wildness and

energy had found its right outlet, and compared with earlier behaviour, I was quiet. Because I no longer wished to turn our house upside down nor wanted to slay its inmates, I found my mother pleased to have me home again. Sighs of thanksgiving must have escaped her when she realized the days of terror and fights with breadknives were over. Even Harry seemed acceptable again, and I saw in him not only an excellent friend for my mother, but the carefree man we children had liked.

I did not notice much of what happened while at home, for the missionary books engrossed me. Most of the adventures they recounted seemed to involve day-long treks. So I did a lot of walking to get myself up to the required standard. My chemist's shop lay over four miles from our house, on the other side of the river in the suburbs. Not once did I go by tram, yet I never failed to be first on the doorstep at nine every morning. Five minutes or so later, Billy the senior assistant would come and open the door. Immediately I got in I had to dash to the switchboard and put the telephone through from the boss's home to the shop, so that from the 'ting' he would know business had begun for the day. Only on conditions of apprenticeship to pharmacy would the chemist take me on, and agreement to this meant that I was strictly banned from serving in the shop, even in rush hours. Billy had the shop entirely to himself until ten o'clock when the boss appeared. Theoretically. But in fact, since Billy went dancing well into the early hours of most mornings, he came to the shop unshaven. While he secluded himself in the cloakroom with a razor, I served in the shop. Life and death, as it were, I dispensed through my own two hands. At that hour of the morning, however, only a few customers came, and mostly for unexciting things like cough lozenges and tins of purée for babies. Joy in this new-found power lasted until the day when a cocky young seaman returned to the shop and gave me such a lecture (plus threats) because he resented the Gospel tract I had slipped into the packet of contraceptives.

Fortunately, the boss's movements were like clockwork, so he never caught me serving. When he arrived I was already busy in the back room. Shelves loaded with antiquated bottles divided this work-space from the shop. Rows and rows of bottles in dark green and dark blue glass made a pleasing display with their luxurious-looking gold labels and names in apothecary's Latin. In this barrier a secret spy-hole had been made, so that I could keep my eye open for would-be stealers of sponges or tiny bottles of perfume.

Our shop specialized in perfume. After we left at night, the boss made it in secret. In the mornings I found a sink full of jars and pots to be washed. Friday night was our big time for selling the perfume, when it went like hot cakes at 'eighteen pence' a go. Pay day at a nearby mill caused this onslaught and the mill girls streamed into the shop on their way home with virgin wage packets. Preparations for their arrival went ahead like a military campaign. We all manned our posts. Mine was with the incense burner loaded with the boss's heady creation. When the first girls rushed in, the shop thoroughly reeked of a sweet, sickly smell. 'The lilac again next week' I would hear the boss announce. Then his bald pate would appear round the barrier expecting me to have another half-gross of the current concoction labelled and corked. None of the girls seemed to mind that we bottled these delectable waters rather crudely. None of the fancy shapes and delicate boxes usually connected with perfume, stood on our counter. And even the bottles we did have, were fitted with outrageously large corks. Only the stuff inside interested the girls, for they knew that the cheap scent acted like pollen to bees in the dockland round about.

Second Blessing

Working in the chemist's had trails of glory, epitomized in the short white jacket I wore. It cloaked me with importance and gave customers the impression that I understood the mystique of medicines. From childhood I remembered the chemist's shop, always so clean-smelling, its assistants so superior as they weighed the howling babies. What went on behind that screen at the back where they disappeared with unintelligible prescriptions, to emerge minutes later with bottles of every imaginable colour? In my innocence I thought it all vaguely connected with those huge pear-shaped bottles, bigger than myself, that stood in the window like red and yellow and green and blue Russian domes. Now, unbelievably, I could come and go at will myself from the screened area and show myself to the customers, taking down the fantastic jars. Monday mornings provided the only time when the white coat could be shown-off outside on official business. Fire-watching headquarters for the whole block of shops was in the chemist's, and I had to go round collecting their financial contributions. The girl assistants were not slow to take advantage of a direct contact with scarce supplies, and soon I retained many on my black-market list. I did not consider this wrong. In Fermanagh, cycling over the border into Eire for occasional smuggling was quite a natural part of the country people's lives, even for the 'saved', for after all that particular law was man-made not God-made. To do similar things at the chemist's seemed no different to me morally.

In spite of its public splendour, in private, behind the barrier, my white coat confined me to a very dull life. Packets of Epsom salts had to be weighed up, the telephone had to be answered, and dozens of queer-looking substances pounded in mortars. A bunsen-burner stood on the bench. This sort of gadget had filled me with excitement in school, but now I could actually get my hands on one, I was only allowed to use it for sealing up parcels. A completely free hand, however, was given me over the cough mixture. A dark winter alternating between biting winds and driving rain, created a big demand for our cough mixture. At the back of the shop, in a recess under the stairs, was an old gas-cooker with a capacious pot. I boiled the carrageen moss in this, intriguing myself for hours by mixing the various juices and spices. It gave me a thrill to walk down the block in my smart white jacket to buy a penny nutmeg at the grocers. I did nothing to minimize my importance in the eyes of the grocer's girl who liked me to get her under-the-counter films.

I liked the carrageen moss, which was not moss at all, but seaweed that had been bleached along the shore. It brought Gertie so much to mind. I could picture her at the daily task of boiling the white moss to make Uncle's favourite milk pudding. And did she not use the fine muslin cloth of the carrageen strainer as handkerchiefs?

Acceptance into the chemist's had been conditional. I promised to study for the pharmaceutical examinations. Every week a minimum number of hours must be devoted to this end. Latin came first, and I duly enrolled at an evening class. But it proved to be no use at all, partly from having too many students, and I learnt almost nothing. But Billy came to the rescue. I discovered that one activity which took place behind the barrier, was the eating of lunch sandwiches long before lunch-time came. This left us a whole hour free to stroll by the Lough coast. Billy's gaiety and provocative humour reminded me of Jack at the paint merchants. Both seemed to delight in knocking away the props holding up staid convention. My new friend certainly had no objection to people gaping as I went by reciting Latin declensions parrot-wise. Billy also set me written exercises and translations, and altogether gave up a great deal of his time for my betterment. For his services he asked nothing, except one thing. Would I, please, stop distributing those ghastly Gospel tracts to everybody we passed in the street, or to those who sat beside us in the transport café where we had a cup of tea?

Acquiescence came more readily than I would admit. Indeed, I felt relieved. Since coming back from Gertie's, wind had been taken out of my religious life's sails. Thoughts lurked that the loveliness of my summer on the farm might not all have been because of salvation's joys. Losing my position as preacher at the little hall might not be the sole reason why I had been sorry to leave. As though the last four months had not existed, my mission hall life in the city had begun again where it left off. Apparently nothing had changed. As before, I attended services in the hall on most nights, and carried one of the scriptural banners in the Sunday street parade. For a time, also, Sadie and her family held on to me as their special protégé and still showed me off like a performing dog to their friends.

A close observer, however, would have discovered fine cracks already disfiguring the enamelled miniature of heaven. Subtle changes had taken place during my absence. Surely I, of all people, should have learnt from my weird and wide experiences, the sad mutability of human affairs. For a long time after my return I could not determine exactly what the change was. Mood rather than incident dominated the atmosphere. Perhaps, after all, the mission hall and its congregation were no different, but only I had changed. Certainly the fire of the Gospel was slaked compared with the first weeks after my 'conversion'. No disbelief or doubt had entered in, but it just seemed hardly worth the effort of shouting and dancing about on platforms if Gertie was not in the congregation to enjoy it all, and smile approval at me.

For instance, I had not written to Phyllis again after meeting the friendly Gertie. She had never replied in my own warm tones, yet now I sensed hauteur in her attitude. But again, to make things even more complicated, she refused to take me seriously. Though fervent herself, my fervour raised the ghost of a smile in her eyes. This irritated me excessively. Above all, I wanted people to take me seriously—especially now that Gertie had regarded me as a man. Let Phyllis laugh, I thought, she may laugh alone. And I began to look elsewhere for a companion.

Incredible taboos were placed upon any open mention of sex. Yet the young men and women of our congregation would not dream of being without 'a little friend' of the opposite sex, neither would the older ones expect them to be. But I, who until autumn had known a bliss that none of the ninnies in the hall would ever know, I must walk alone. My heart belonged very much to Gertie. She still possessed all the qualities I could want in a woman. Yet I could say nothing about her, not even mention her name. And this was not only on account of her age and her son's, who was three years older than I was, but on account of my own. Perhaps I never regretted the contradiction between my years and looks more than over my love for Gertie. How I longed to be over twenty one!

If I did not choose a 'Christian' friend from the flock, and show every sign of settling down to a 'steady', like all the other young men, people would begin to whisper. But I need not have bothered my head about gossip, for they shortly began to whisper anyway, although about other matters. Amongst the younger fry where I began to make sorties, I found a wariness among the girls. Being 'saved' did not help me much. I began to think that by nefarious means they had learnt of my wildness during 'pre-conversion' days, and decided to keep out of the terror's way. Then adolescent inferiority struck at me, and I imagined my pimples kept the girls at bay. I plagued Billy for ointments. St. Valentine's Day brought me a shock. Seven cards plopped on to the front door mat at home. Despite the 'worldly' messages inside (they certainly had not been bought at the Bible depot as all cards should) and the absence of names, I guessed mission hall girls had sent them. No other girls I knew would write anything as sloppy as 'your broken-hearted peach' which I found on one card.

Seven! Well, that gave me a clue and I set about to track down the senders. With luck I would soon have someone to take along to conventions and missions. Gertie, I felt sure, would have quite understood. At the Friday prayer-meeting following St. Valentine's Day, I realized without doubt that one of my admirers was Marjorie, She always attended with her mother and elder sister, the girls being noticeable for their magnificent golden hair, and expensive-looking camel-hair coats. Their mother was also well-dressed, too much so, I considered, in that Persian lamb coat which somehow had a touch of the 'world' about it. This family trio were all 'saved' and prayed well at the Friday meeting. Yet they kept very much to themselves and managed quite successfully to convey the impression that they were a cut above you.

On that Friday, however, I gave Marjorie a good old-fashioned what's-what with my eye as she came in. From another source I had found out that she was seventeen, and therefore well within range. Whether naturally or not I could not tell, but she blushed most attractively and went ahead with her sister. Modestly, they took their usual place on a bench across the way from mine. Half-way through the second hymn, I saw her looking at me. Before the prayer requests had been read out, our eyes had made all the arrangements necessary for me to walk her home. But as soon as we got together, I became tongue-tied and embarrassed. Close-to, Marjorie was prettier than even at a distance. Evidently she was rich also, for their house had two bay windows.

Unnoticed at first, spring's harbingers had come. The lime-tree lined road where Marjorie and I walked lent itself eminently to romance. But still I could do nothing except talk about 'the Call' and the salvation of other souls. How different the walk would be, I kept reminding myself, if Gertie had been there. Nevertheless, Marjorie consented to come with me on Saturday night to the big mission down town. For evangelicals, going to any kind of large religious gathering in the city, had all the air of theatre-going which the 'ungodly' enjoyed. Best clothes came out, and tea might be taken in select restaurants. Suitably spruced up then, on the following night I presented myself at Marjorie's door, and found to my horror, her mother all ready to go with us. I had not bargained for that. We set out briskly, armed with pencils and paper, the two women's faces ruddy with nothing more sinful than 'God's water and soap'.

When the meeting finished, I spotted Sadie and Phyllis. They had been on the ground floor while we perched in the gallery. I waved and grinned at them. Phyllis did not answer at all, and Sadie gave me the coldest of responses. Ideas that Phyllis might be jealous of Marjorie would not bear scrutiny, for Phyllis must have known perfectly well how much more at ease I would have been in her own mature company. Ever since my 'conversion', a custom had sprung up of my eating Sunday dinner with Sadie's family. Before going to Gertie's, this had suited me well for it kept me away from my own home throughout the whole day. And even now, when things were happy at home, the arrangement saved me a long cross-city walk home and back again. Using a Sunday tram was entirely out of the question.

After the breaking-of-bread next morning, I made my way through the crush as usual, to find Sadie and her family. Phyllis intercepted me and sarcastically supposed that Marjorie's mother would be giving me Sunday dinner *that* day. Obviously, Phyllis had been thinking out a wounding remark since the night before. She certainly timed it well. Before I recovered from this uncalled-for attack, Phyllis disgorged everything that poisoned her. It was extremely petty, but then these people allowed few large issues to enter their lives. Indoor decorating at Marjorie's house had caused it all. Sadie's brother had done the work and, apparently, not to the satisfaction of Marjorie's mother. Ending up in most un-Christian-like scenes, the two families had not been on speaking terms since. Phyllis indicated now that I must choose definitely which camp I wanted to be in. If I forsook them for the others, not only would I never share Scripture Union Notes round the fire with Sadie and family, but in the mission hall, I must cross to Marjorie's bench.

I did not know whether to be more amazed or amused at this childish behaviour. But it focused my attention on the question of unity. And when I looked at the strong walls of our citadel, behold, cracks rent them from the foundation to battlements. From the two factions between them whom I must choose, I looked elsewhere in the congregation and found similar rifts. And the more I analysed events there, the more splits could be detected. There was a whole hierarchy of not-speaking-to, only-on-nodding-terms-with, mustn't-be-sat-next-to, and other forms of Thank-God-I'm-not-as-this-man behaviour. But then how could our hall be otherwise? It had been founded on schism. In the 'old' hall something 'unsound' was said by the preacher. A dozen of the congregation stood up in the middle of the sermon and stalked out. Others followed and they built a new hall—the one where I was 'born again'. Shortly after my arrival in the midst, our own hall went through similar convulsions. The leading elder went off with a slice of our congregation. A newcomer, a most outstanding 'soul-winner', threatened to overshadow the elder's personality, and rather than be eclipsed he took himself off with supporters too. Differences of this magnitude could not be hid, especially as the two fragments of congregation met in buildings on the same road. In fairness, it must be said that this unfounded division smote the conscience of some. When pleas for 'revival' went forth at prayer-meetings, these people expressed their willingness to catch fire from any source—'even up the road, Lord'.

Forced by Phyllis to choose, I did so. For a few Sundays, Marjorie's mother gave me my Sunday dinner. Unfortunately fine though their lime avenue became with growing spring, no deep romance developed beneath its leaves, between Marjorie and me. I sat with her now in the mission hall, and hardly exchanged glances with Phyllis. Sadie was so engulfed with the happiness of her new married life, that she smiled at all and sundry, probably without knowing who they were. Her eyes now were only for her husband. Marjorie bored me. For as long as possible, I spun things out. But in the end I gave her up. One night instead of walking her along the lime avenue, I left her at the end with the inevitable excuse 'It's not the Lord's will'. On other evenings I began to go home immediately the services ended, in order to avoid her. And last of all, I had to use drastic measures. As she was the clinging type, I stopped going to the mission hall so often.

The schisms had already undermined my faith in the hall's theological position. I felt no loss except perhaps the public speaking platform which had become so necessary to me. Immediately my attendance faltered, various parties began to impugn me as a 'backslider'. Suspicions were confirmed, for I now spent most evenings fire-watching to amass more precious cash towards my missionary training. Though I forsook that particular mission hall, I still had fervent faith in 'the Call'. Being a 'backslider' I could bear, but I refused to become a backbiter. Sweet-natured Gertie had instilled that into me. Whatever faults may have been hers, small-mindedness was not one.

Fire-watching proved to be less rigorous than sitting for hours on wooden benches, making or listening to interminable prayers. We had no drill to do, except keep buckets of sand and water ready by the stirrup-pumps, and be generally prepared to cope with a shower of German incendiary bombs. Charts were pinned up showing us how to douse them. The draper's dilapidated attic we used as sleeping quarters, looked particularly inflammable. Fortunately, not so much as a spark touched it during my term of office. Only when the sirens sounded the 'alert' were we expected to show active signs of readiness. Meanwhile, Goldilocks-like, I could make a choice between three iron bedsteads and their complement of hard mattresses and army blankets now as tattered as scarecrows. Choice of beds fell to me because none of the other fire-watchers used them. Their nights passed entirely with drinking and card-playing in the next room, or dozing in the derelict armchairs. I could hear them through the rickety partition once hung with wallpaper. In one place, I could see a chink of light where plaster had fallen from the wooden studding. Long silences, when I could hear nothing except the clink of bottles, would end suddenly with yells of triumph, groans of defeat, laughter and the noise of money changing hands. At first I left Gospel tracts in their room— slipped into a pack of cards, between the leaves of a newspaper, or under beer bottles. But this soon stopped when I found they devoured an enormous number every week by using them as cigarette spills.

During this period, while my hall attendances trickled like a drying-up stream, I would go straight from the services to the draper's attic. Sometimes another young 'brother' would accompany me. Together we would put on the gas-fire that stayed alight until morning, make tea, and before he departed for his home nearby, pray for the defeat of Satan under that fire-susceptible roof. Then our duty rota changed, and one night a new fire-watcher did come into the room to lie down. I heard nothing until I woke up in confusion. For a moment I could not remember where I was, nor whether a dream or an external noise disturbed me. First in my bemused state I wondered if the Lord had indeed arrived on His daily-prayed-for Second Coming, for the air was full of music. The sound seemed to ascend and descend simultaneously. The sonorous melody repeated and echoed like thunder in vast canyons of cloud.

'Drown that bloody row' from the card-room brought me from the trance.

The Lord had not come, but only the new fire-watcher with a large wireless from which poured the *Sanctus* of Bach's *B Minor Mass*. In answer he turned it up even louder, until the noble structure of sound threatened to shake slates off the roof and the remaining plaster from the partition. When the *Sanctus* ended he turned the volume control down again and gave me a solemn wink across the fire-lit room. 'Do them good' he whispered. And apart from that he did not speak again until the *Mass* ended. Then he told me, in answer to my question, that Bach wrote the music over two hundred years ago for celebration of the mass.

How much more could an evangelical like me, stomach in one evening? In loyalty to my calling, I should have jumped out of bed immediatly on hearing the music and switched off the 'Devil's box'. Believing Satan to be 'Prince of the air', many 'keener' members of our mission hall thought that radio waves and the Devil were almost synonymous. They refused to have radios in their houses, and never listened to one, for fear of being contaminated by relayed sin. Not only had I failed in this duty, but I had actually listened to music for a mass! Could sin ever be more scarlet than mine? Instead of craving the Lord's forgiveness, I leant back against the pillow, still thrilled with my new musical discovery, and listening as the new fire-watcher told me about the following night's concert. I did not feel the slightest guilt. Over Gertie, too, I had been forced to adjust an unrelenting theology to fit my own needs. I adopted the delightful heresy that whatsoever seemed beautiful to me, must also be good. I remembered too, the way in which people at the mission hall prayed at length about unity and love and then five minutes later set about dividing and hating. If believing one thing but doing another was a sin, at least I was not alone in wrong-doing.

More radical than these niceties of evangelical argument, however, was the jolt Bach gave me. For many months now I had been starved of music. Although not knowing much about it, at least I realized music could get deep down inside of you, touching cords of tenderness or sadness as nothing else could. The mission hall had led me to think that any music other than its own poverty-stricken wailing was wrong. Instead of bread they gave me stones, serpents instead of fish. How sick I had grown of Gospel hymn-tunes and their saccharin sweetness, their prosaic harmonies and flat-footed rhythms. Our street procession always set off with 'Marching beneath the banner', a reasonable hymn with an emetic melody. Parading with scriptural texts itself never caused me embarrassment, but what a fool I felt at many of those grisly hymns. Had our devotional singing been that of the old Florentine *Laudi Spirituali*, it might have been worth while, and certainly have gained us attention.

My final break with the mission hall, home of my 'conversion' could not be delayed now. When they knew that instead of praying with them, I was listening to concerts on the 'Devil's box' every night, the end came. To be rid of party warfare caused me no distress. Deeply religious feelings remained, and in spite of the congregation's opinion, I numbered myself amongst the 'elect' because of being 'saved'. 'Backsliding into the world' was far from my intention, for that would mean the end of my missionary adventures. Now that I lived contentedly at home, I could go to halls nearer our street—halls in fact like Stanley's.

I found it on my way home from the chemist's one evening. A poster outside announced a series of meetings for believers. In smaller print underneath was a man's name, as principal of a missionary training college. I dived into the hall to make sure of a seat, for here was somebody who could surely help me. He would have a message specially for me! His sermon dealt with the Holy Ghost's work in the Christian life. And this membership in the fuller life could not be enjoyed by those whose baptism was only of 'blood'. (How underprivileged he made us sound, those who were merely 'saved'.) 'No, brethren,' he continued, 'we are called to another baptism.' I sat on the seat edge almost sweating with curiosity. 'The baptism of fire.' Well that was exciting enough, and sounded worth having. The principal explained how those truly receiving this baptism should show it—by raising a hand, just as we did at the baptism of 'blood', getting 'saved'. He finished and to soft hymn-singing he pleaded with the congregation. Was there nobody present who would show that they had taken the Holy Ghost into their lives? Of course, I plainly saw now what had hindered further development in my spiritual life, what had held me back from turning off the wireless, lack of this Second Blessing. If only for the poor 'black folk's' sake, I dearly wanted to serve the Lord.

So I put my hand up. Singing stopped for the usual commendatory 'Amens'. Then I noticed that my hand was not alone like a periscope above the sea of faces. Across the hall, a young man's hand stuck up. I could just make out the blond head the hand belonged to. It was Stanley's.

CHAPTER XI

Spring Fervour

What emotions overwhelmed me on receiving the gift of Second Blessing? None. It was like getting a present of money, you just had to wait for an opportunity to spend it. I did not expect anything bright or beautiful to happen there and then in the hall. And later on, I was too absorbed in the Little Lady to worry.

Stanley's name for his grandmother, suited her perfectly. She picked her way through the heavy Victorian furniture like a poodle in a warehouse. During the week, she wore a dress of red velvet. Much lace hid a neck that must have been young and graceful before the Boer War. Wound many times under the lace and then falling in long loops to her waist, were multicoloured beads. Pinned to the red velvet bosom was the biggest cameo imaginable. Somehow it struck a 'worldly' note on that pious, flat chest, for its white figures in relief were more robust and far less shrouded than the Little Lady's figure itself.

From a massive cupboard in a high-ceilinged bedroom, out came a purple dress for Sundays. This was the day for her single outing of the week—a visit to the mission hall. Other trips during the week were beyond her strength, for she was a very old lady indeed. This could not be denied, however

erect that head of hers might be carried, with its crown of
purest white hair, pinned up like a crisp-baked cottage-loaf.
She was loved by all who knew her. From somewhere inside
the lace-frothy throat, issued out a tiny voice full of sweet
tones like temple bells. It certainly went well with the cameo
and beads, and the ankle-length dresses. Yet few ever stopped
to talk with her. They hated both to draw attention to themselves and to desecrate the Sabbath by shouting. And shout
you must by might and main, if any words at all were to be
conveyed down the ear-trumpet. The clearest diction, the
plainest syntax, roared fortissimo into the metal maw, produced but the faintest effect on her inner ear. Her bright birdy
little eyes darted about, seeking to make coherent the few
sounds actually trapped by the trumpet.

The Little Lady read lips when listening was imperative.
But in the house I always wrote everything down for her.
Stanley was enormously pleased for he gave great devotion to
the old lady, the last of his nearest family. Following on my
Second Blessing and kinship with Stanley, came increasingly
frequent visits to the house. In the end, I had my supper with
them almost every evening and often spent week-ends there.
Very soon to my Second Blessing I could add a second home,
to which I was given a key. The Little Lady knew the time of
our arrival back from the services, and would be peeping
through the thick lace curtains to see us open the gate. She
greeted us with one of her familiar expressions. It might be,
'The Evil One's been abroad all night!' delivered in a suitably
awed voice. Friendliness faded from the little eyes and a glaze
of fear slid over them. We knew what that meant. Pointing
ceilingwards, indicating the rooms above, she would whisper
with horror, 'Winebibbing!' Yes, the student lodgers had
again taken 'liquid refreshment' into their rooms. The Little
Lady's nose compensated her defunct ears. Where the smell

of alcohol was concerned, it was as sharp as a red-setter's.

Stanley's age and mine differed by eleven years. He had a 'testimony' stretching back to childhood, when he was 'saved' at a children's service on the sands of Down. But though younger than he, I took the lead in public. I could face any street-corner service with a bold, brazen confidence. But Stanley blushed even when asked questions by American soldiers to whom he handed tracts. And neither had he got 'the Call', though he was expecting it. Physically too, Stanley felt overawed by me. Neither the Little Lady nor he could believe that my sixteenth birthday had still to come, for I towered amongst the weighty mahogany furniture making it almost human in scale. The draught-curtain behind the sitting-room door was pulled back and my height recorded on the frame. My photograph was installed on the mantel-piece along with those of other missionaries already 'in the field'. For most of these, the 'field' was China, as evidenced by other pictures in the room. Sunsets over harbours crammed with junks had gilt Chinese characters spattered on them. 'Texts,' said the Little Lady when she first found me examining them. But there were so many, I doubted whether she knew which of them was John 3: 16, or Romans 10: 9.

Stanley's shortcomings were insignificant when seen against his stature in 'personal evangelism'. He was colossal. Though he might be small in size, and brief in testimony he gave when forced to do so at outdoor services, when witnessing alone he became a positive Spurgeon. Whether it was because his grandmother brought him up I could never tell, but Stanley's success in life undoubtedly lay with the old ladies. On three nights of the week and for many hours on Sunday, he went into the hospitals and homes for the aged. I think it was not only the case-loads of food that made him welcome at these bedsides, but his cheerful Nordic face. He kept names and addresses of all these people, the city's unwanted flotsam, in a book and tried to trace family or friends for them. But though his kindness was unsparing and genuine, his main concern was to get the old ladies 'saved' at the eleventh hour. The first night I met him coming out of the main hospital, tears still ran beside his nose—someone had 'come through on the Lord's side' a mere hour before dying. A brand snatched indeed from the burning in a matter of minutes! We went into a corner for a quick thanksgiving.

Stanley slaved unremittingly at this work. His fever of 'personal evangelism' was contagious. Soon I found myself immersed in his work also. But I preferred visiting the families at their homes to bending over the dying in hospital beds. Many of these old people passed their last days in iron cots, with bars to prevent them falling on to the floor. No wonder they grew cantankerous. Pleasing them demanded not only charm and patience, but firmness too. Stanley possessed just the right blend, and performed magnificently. Obstinacy and indifference melted at his touch. What a lot he could teach me, I thought, for my future life. 'Black folk' probably required nothing very much different in the way of help and comfort, from other folk. Roughly an equal amount of time had to be spent at each of the old people's beds, otherwise unfortunate jealousies and accusations of favouritism arose. Exceptions, of course, were at bedsides where the 'Spirit was working' within a soul.

Social propriety existed amongst the old dames, which we had to keep. Some of the women retained pride to the end, and would never allow themselves to be called anything other than Mrs. Smith. Yet others delighted to be just plain Nellie—even at ninety. Old Lizzie was undoubtedly the most ancient. She had seen all eighteen of her children buried. Every week Lizzie would tell you that she was 'almost a-mended' and hoped to be back with her flower basket by the City Hall soon. Hope! It was the last remaining thing a lot of the poor crones had on this earth. Some, when they lost it, died forthwith, but others even then, clung to life though it had no more to offer them. No wonder eternity, the eternity which alone could make a pattern from the scattered bits, became almost tangible at times.

But it seemed impossible for old Lizzie to die. Despite decrepitude, a live spark burned inside. She had not the slightest intention of giving up. She looked as though quite prepared to snatch the scythe from Death's hand when he came stalking the wards. At our first meeting, she was up to all her old tricks, and tried to get me to smuggle her in a supply of snuff. Much winking and rambling on to other topics was involved in her explanation. When, however, I gave her a parcel of cakes at the next visit, instead of the desired snuff, she grew quite haughty and threw them back at me. Stanley came to the rescue. He clapped his hands in disapproval and told Lizzie how cross he was. How could she treat his good rock cakes like that—cakes that he had sat up so late last night to make for her? Her withered old head dropped then, and the tears flowed in contrition. But they soon dried up again with the singing of 'Climb, climb up sunshine mountains'. Stanley's powers of persuasion would never be mine, I thought enviously. Yet I must strive to attain them. 'Personal evangelism' was so very essential.

Getting currants and raisins and other rationed ingredients for the food parcels, was my best contribution to Stanley's pastoral work among the aged. Gertie did not fail me. Butter arrived in what for war-time were astonishing quantities. And occasionally the post van would deliver cold things in sacks that when clipped open proved to be ducks or chickens. From Fermanagh large boxes of spring flowers arrived, as fresh as when Maggie packed them in the layers of moss. All these good things showered on Stanley's house, for the gift parcels were made up there. My usual black-market prices could not be charged, of course, because the things were in 'the Lord's service'. Perhaps I did even better out of it by donation. Whenever a new load came, the Little Lady would lift up her velvet skirt and fumble about in her petticoats for a hidden pocket full of notes. Besides tapping the sources for provisions, I could also assist Stanley in his baking. With pride I told him how I had baked the bread on one farm where I stayed as an evacuee. Stanley's trepidation vanished when my first batch came deliciously out of the oven. We endeavoured to fill six trays each containing a dozen cakes at a baking. But if I had mulcted my country contacts of extra fat, two more trays could be managed. The Little Lady never interfered. But when our baking was done she would come daintily into the kitchen, eyes aglow as she counted the cakes. 'Eighty-four,' she would exclaim in childish delight, 'praise the Lord. *Jehovah jireh*.'

Easter came, and with it the greatest blessings so far called down on me by the Little Lady. The Easter eggs caused this. Stanley's grandmother had done our kind of visiting herself during more than forty of her active years. Normal plans for Easter, however, were disrupted by the war, for they had centred around eggs. Before 'that nasty man', as she called Hitler, raped Europe, she used to collect a mountain of eggs, and paint texts on them. At Easter time she then distributed them to her 'sick folk'. A more superior way of 'getting the message over' she considered, than her lavender sachets with texts. That year's egg plans were hatched one evening, when the Little Lady realized I could probably get enough eggs to make the thing worth while. Well in advance, I warned Maggie and Gertie of what our needs would be. They replied with the usual interest and promised the eggs in time for painting. Alas! both parcels from Fermanagh and Antrim arrived in a sorry mess. The Little Lady's eyes began to brim, her mouth to quiver. That she should weep from disappointment was more than I could bear. There was no alternative but for me to go personally all the way to Gertie's. When she sent presents of eggs to her 'unsaved' relations, she herself wrote texts on them as a means of witness. My demand for extra dozens would doubtless leave her short, a fact to be concealed from Uncle. Yet I knew Gertie would give me all I needed if the hens were laying.

Mere thought of my journey aroused the most gratifying sensations. Thinking about Gertie was like trying to recall exactly the scent of a rose, or the first plunge into the sea early on a summer morning. I knew they were beautiful, but no amount of day-dreaming could thrill like the real thing. Gertie was seldom out of my thoughts. But now I was to find her again, my whole body was tense with emotion. The bus that bumped along the coast roads, seemed to be pulled by a half-dead horse instead of an engine. Inside, the windows steamed up, and to see out I had to keep clearing the glass, like a hole in ice. But I had no need of windows, for instinct told me when we got to the stop at the crossroads. Once down, I ran headlong towards the moor. Nobody at the farm knew I was coming. A postcard would have brought Leslie down with the trap to meet me, and then he would have monopolized my day, making it difficult to see Gertie about the eggs. No, it was far better to stumble on Gertie unannounced. I knew the farm routine never varied, and geared my walk across the moor to coincide with Uncle's rising from the pitch. Gertie would be alone then.

A fine wind off the sea fanned the moor grasses, and I breathed deep of the mingled ozone and smell of damp earth.

A blithe atmosphere seemed to have already transformed the winter landscape. Far hills and woods looked ready for summer again. Behind and below me was the cove of so many memories. Waves were racing in. I remembered the summer, the heated pebbles where I stood while Gertie dried me. At the cove I had persuaded her to take off the Edwardian boots and paddle in a pool. I looked back but no one was there now. There never was. The sea rode into the cove in ridges, not wildly, though powerfully nevertheless. But they broke, licked up the shore, touching the thick harvest of seaweed left by the high tides. In spite of the spring day with the year's first hint of summer to come, I thought the little cove looked sad. Only the waders had halcyon hours now amongst the wrack. Could our love be forgotten, just as our footprints were long washed from the sand, as cold and dead as the ancient fires of the kelp-burners?

I dropped down. Leaping the well-sheugh, I heard the sound of Gertie's buckets. She was drawing water, and singing to herself. In a flash she was mine. All mine. Our love was as changeless as the waves below in the tangle cove.

At Easter, faith broke out like a rash. The Second Blessing mission hall reached a pitch of hysteria which almost blossomed into the long-awaited 'revival'. Everyone was astonished at the numbers 'coming forth', and even believers themselves woke like volcanoes from slumber. We were all 'on fire'. The usual run of services and meetings could not satisfy our burning spirits. Extra prayer-meetings took place late at night. Our day's labour in the 'world' could not be faced without yet more prayer-meetings before going to work. And who minded getting up early on those spring mornings? Sunlight fell on the city's grand civic buildings, refacing their winter façades with new colour and texture. You could even see the pigeon's shadows, where the birds perched along an over-ornate cornice. And although it rained, when the clouds parted we looked up at radiant blue. Even the older ones among us felt the touch of youth in their limbs again. God's created world seemed to be in harmony for once with His promises of glory to come. It was good, when your head was bent in prayer, to feel a strong ray of sunshine on your neck.

Belfast had nearly come to 'revival' during the previous year. A big tent campaign was held on a blitzed site in the city centre. Rumours flew round now of another threatened conflagration. The halls and churches just simply would not squeeze everybody in if the whole city turned to the Lord. Rather than dissipate our strength on coals not yet alight, we stoked the humble fire of our own hall. That at least, we felt convinced, was the genuine thing. One of the chief stokers was Perry, a student from the missionary college headed by the Second Blessing director. In fact he had completed his training, and was almost at the end of a short course on tropical medicine before going to Africa. Perry had devoted his Easter vacation to the work at our hall, and was staying with Stanley and the Little Lady. It was therefore inevitable that the hero of the hour, a missionary-to-be, should shine brighter for me than the humble Stanley.

Perry quickly took me under his wing, and I made him my pattern. His 'Call', his unhesitating answer to it, his uncomplicated vision of duty before him, his certainty, were most appealing. These characteristics stood out in strong outlines, so different from Stanley's slower, more cautious approach to life. At that time I was too inexperienced to see which of them possessed the subtler, gentle nature, where seeds of love rather than conquest were sown. Perry vanquished me. Round his person the aura of Africa glowed already. After Easter, Perry would go back to his hospital for just six weeks.

And then. . . . Envy gripped me so that I hardly dared to think of the *then*. He would board a boat. He would sail tranquilly south. He would trek into the jungle. And on every side the drums of Africa would roll in welcome to the lucky Perry. Of course, there could be no question now of my not doing my training at his college, and following him hotfoot to the 'field'.

The spark of 'revival' failed to ignite the city. Many times the flint struck but the tinder would not catch. Disappointment in our hearts, we watched the spiritual eruption subside. Crowds eased off. You could sit on your mission hall bench without your neighbours hams and elbows digging you. And towards the end, there was no longer any need to arrive half an hour before meetings, in order to get your usual place. But we kept feelings of failure to ourselves. Our cheerfulness was greater than before though noticeably forced. 'Christians' never acknowledged defeat, not when we knew the final victory would be ours. So off we went to the Bangor Convention to seek blessings there.

Belfast dockers might not be marching to their work shouting Gospel hymns, as we had hoped they would, yet we could turn the train bearing us away to Bangor into a 'Hallelujah Express'. No wonder the other passengers got cross. They could neither read the paper nor dream quietly out of the window, for our choruses pierced every eardrum. But we had one railway carriage contact that led to 'conversion', even if the Devil went about like a roaring lion. He tried to get indignant sinners to stop our hymn-singing. Of course the ringing tones of goodness and mercy caused them discomfort. But they had no right to interfere. My blood boiled when a schoolboy laconically enquired as to why didn't we dry up. And I could have murdered him when he insulted my hero personally.

'Blatherskite'.

What a thing to say to *my* Perry who was arduously at work on the soul to be 'saved'. Then the schoolboy exhaled jets of cigarette smoke at him in such a supercilious way—at Perry, whose great point in his 'testimony' was that he used to smoke thirty cigarettes a day and even had his shirts tailored!

The spring I had first sensed under the lime trees with Marjorie had reached its prime. Each of its voluptuous days brought the key event of my life nearer, my sixteenth birthday. By now all my inner hopes and fears had been confided to Perry. There was no part of my mind or soul to which he did not have access, though I never told him about Gertie. And if anything was needed to confirm my unstinted worship of him, he did it now. Perry gloriously agreed that it might just be possible for me to make my training application after that birthday. Meanwhile there were hundreds of pursuits to occupy our days. Since Perry was proceeding to Africa on nothing but 'faith' (that is without guaranteed financial support) we prayed at all meetings for the Lord to open His garner. And sure enough, anonymous letters were delivered at Stanley's house, containing large sums of money. A registered letter came with a hundred pounds as his passage money.

Stanley and I bought Perry an enormous wooden trunk from Smithfield Market. Its rows of rivets and domed lid looked most impressive. In spite of its age, a bit of cleaning brought the surface up like new, making our missionary a vastly strong box. Stanley stencilled the new owner's name on it, and Mark 16: 15 underneath. Having these things about was tantalizing to me. I could bear the idea of Perry going away and having the marvellous life that I wanted for myself. But when new clothes were put in the trunk the reality of the whole thing made me jealous. I wanted to be leaving myself for heathen shores so much, that almost physical pain resulted. Could I steal away, hidden in the box, be loaded, shipped, and unloaded, without discovery? Wilder things than that had been planned in my time. Although my legs were long, I could fit neatly in the box, and even be comfortable when the lid was down. Perry merely laughed. Would I get out please, as he had clothes to put in. Tropical suits had also been supplied miraculously (in answer to prayer of course). When nobody else was looking, I fingered the fine material enviously, wondering what shiny black hands would care for them under the rolling sun of Africa.

Excitements crowded thick on each other during that spring. On one of its loveliest days, we held our Sunbeam outing. Perry led fifty children out of the city, like a Pied Piper. A long chain of chattering kids found its way out of the streets to the beechwoods beyond, along the river Lagan's banks. Once we were free of the trams, away went Perry at the head, almost dancing as he played his accordion. He performed beautifully—at least, that was my opinion. His slender fingers flew about the keyboard, plucking every known fruit from the evangelical cornucopia of four-line choruses. Music floated across the meadows as we came to the beeches. Neither Perry, nor any of the Sunbeams, realized that this outing was a sentimental journey for me. What memories those favourite woods held. Curving gracefully as the river curved, rising loftily from the water's edge to a pillared skyline, the beechwoods had been a paradise for me when I was ten. But I had not been to them now for years, not since before evacuation to the West country. Now the woods looked small, almost amateur. The fine forests of Fermanagh spoiled me for anything else.

The beechwoods did not disappoint me. Coming back

from the country to the city again had taught me how even
eternal things change. I was merely curious about the woods.
Now as they rang with the children's shouts and laughter I
looked for familiar boles. Most that I had known still stood,
despite being burnt out hollow by our camp fires. Not the
woods, but only I had changed. I was expanding, growing
beyond the earlier pattern, just as the initials and hearts were
doing, carved on the tree trunks so long ago. The beeches
could hold me no longer. Pellucid layer on layer of leaves,
still edged with the daintiest fringes of gossamer, could offer
me no grateful shade. Only the tropical paradise of dense
jungle occupied a place in my imagination now. The gentle,
noble beeches vanished from my mind's eye, I saw only the
scarlet flame tree on fire, and smelt the voluptuous scent of
frangipani falling on the dusk air.

Waiting. I seemed to spend my entire days waiting. Even
the years of training were an abyss separating me from the
day of departure. No wonder Perry could race about on that
fine spring day and radiate happiness as bright as the sun itself.
His trunk was practically packed. Nevertheless, the enjoyment going on all around me, banished my moodiness. For a
time I forgot about jungle drums and picked bluebells and
purple charlies instead, with the children. Even the most
pious got tired of chorus singing, and abandoned themselves
to sunshine, or allowed beguiling bird-song to lure them into
the bramble-thickets. Perry flew about everywhere, heart
and soul of the party. He forgot nobody. The girls made him
their darling, the boys their idol. They put flowers in his
black hair, and had they been bobbysoxers and not Sunbeams, they would probably have stripped him.

The children also held races with Perry down to the stream
to get water. No outing could go long without tea and lemon-
ade and things to eat. While Perry and his kids gambolled

about like fauns, the older boys helped me to collect wood. They brought whole green branches, and looked crestfallen when I told them we only wanted to boil saucepans, not the River Lagan itself. On the flattest piece of ground he could find, Stanley looked really at home, milking and sugaring the rows of cups. The whole outing was threatened with disaster and an abrupt end, when a small girl interfered with the fire. In a flash, the pan of hot water emptied itself over her foot. Fortunately, the water was not boiling. But her screams brought everyone running towards the fire—my fire, of course. When the panic had subsided, and the children's interest had been deflected elsewhere, I sat by the dying fire brooding again. The little girl had been rushed to hospital, leaving me in misery with a guilty feeling. I was glad when we all trooped into Belfast again at the end of the day. The dozens of brats scampered away from the hall, all eager to tell Ma about Maisie Jennings getting scalded.

I was pleased to get home myself, for it was Saturday, always a difficult night. The kitchen, the gas-stove, and the tin tub all had to be free simultaneously, if I hoped to get a bath. On that night nobody kept me waiting, and I was already in bed, deliciously fresh and warm, when my mother called up the stairs, 'A big fella at the door for ya.' It was an unorthodox time for anybody to come for me. It might be police about Maisie. But I found Perry downstairs. None of my evangelical associates had ever called at our house before. We did not live in their part of the city. I was confused at Perry's discovery of my home, but I did not expect him to go up to my own room. At heart I was deeply ashamed to let him see how we lived. But Perry could navigate any rocky situation. He did not seem to notice our old furniture or the missing stair-rods. He even laughed when the gas went out without so much as a sigh, and Big 'Ina came up in search of a penny. Perry's visit, however, had weightier things behind it than being merely social. His keys had dropped in the woods while romping with the children. Would I go back there with him in the morning and look for them? I gladly consented, overjoyed because the Sunday was going to be his last full day with us. Not that I could think seriously about my hero leaving, for I had no doubt that I would join him in Africa later.

Recovering from the shock of Perry's call, I brought out the missionary things I had been collecting in a trunk of my own. They were put away against the day when I should sail, when Belfast was nothing but a memory, and even the training was over. No bride ever gave such care and love to her trousseau as I gave to hoarding equipment for my future life. Proudly I lifted out the things to show Perry. I had never allowed any-one else to see them. He hurt me rather by laughing at Gertie's ram's horn ink-stand. My little topee was more successful and took his fancy. In many books about missionary work and travels, I read about malaria and other tropical diseases. My collection therefore included a mosquito net. Sometimes, for special thrills, I tied it to the gas bracket and slept underneath the muslin tent all night. After all I had 'the Call', there was no turning back now. Carefully I laid my things back in their box again, disappointed that Perry had made no expert comments. Anybody could laugh at an old inkstand.

After that, we ran out of things to say, so Perry left, re-minding me again about tomorrow's key-hunt. Fitful showers punctuated Sunday's weather. Between the rain it was hot again as for the children's outing. But Perry took no notice of the rain. We had to shelter under dripping door-ways and then farther out of the city, under scarcely-water-proof trees. But Perry's high spirits showed no signs of abating. When the sun came streaming out again from ragged clouds, Perry stepped out, dodging puddles, every fibre of him declaring 'I *told* you it would be all right'. Of course, for me the road was not the one by the Lagan, leading out to Shaw's Bridge, but a jungle track, where lions lurked. Under those conditions, too, I knew Perry would be his usual cheerful self. What a lot he had taught me, I thought, in the short time he had been with us. That I did my thinking in missionary's terms, and looked at life now from that point of view, was a habit caught from Perry. The taste of professionalism did not displease me. Only the training was needed now to equip me with the remaining jargon and mannerisms. I felt especially grateful to Perry as we approached the Lagan towpath.

Then suddenly, he switched abruptly from our topic of Africa and the 'field'. The river flowed softly against the old towpath bank in lazy swirls. Fish biting the surface, occasionally made rings of ripples, but the current swept them on before they could develop. Then while my dreams were still translating the Lagan idyll into a crocodile-infested swamp, a girl passed us, her arms round a youth. We had noticed them in the distance, as they trailed aimlessly along the riverside, swishing at the grass with a dead stick. I knew her. She lived in our street at home and when we were children, she had been one of those to come into our entry tents to play 'hospitals'. More serious forms of 'fun' obviously occupied her now. We could tell, somehow, that they had lain buried in each other's arms under a tree in the woods, their blood fired by the day's sensuousness. Too involved with each other, they would have passed us without a word. I, also, was too busy with crocodiles to worry about the young couple. But not Perry. Out had to come a Gospel tract. He saw me nod at the girl, and pounced. How did I know a girl like that, who was clearly an 'unsaved' sinner? With the skill of a Grand Inquisitor, Perry prised from me the story of the past. He even had to be told the details of what we had done in the entry as children. Horror filled his eyes.

We stopped, climbed through a barbed-wire fence, and walked towards the picnic wood. For a moment, we went in silence, then Perry began again with his how, why, when, where, with-whom of my sin. The lost keys were no longer important. Before we even reached the wood, where the keys were lost, Perry took hold of my lapels. He faced me squarely. There was no escaping the demand of those dilating moonstone eyes. Had I, he asked boring into me with his intense expression, had I touched a female since my 'conversion'? The question stung me, went down into my soul like iodine on a gashed finger. My love for Gertie could not be denied. I dropped my glance as I confessed.

While these dramatics were going on, a part of my mind detached itself. It hovered about looking down on the accusing Perry and the ashamed me. And this detached bit tried to tell me that for several days Perry's manner towards me had changed. His friendliness seemed less profuse. And this had coincided with his return from Antrim. Because he was going out to the 'field' in 'faith', Perry wanted as many preaching engagements as possible, so that prayers and purses would follow him on the way. With more enthusiasm than tact, I had asked Leslie to invite him to their hall. Naturally, Gertie wanted him home to tea. But Perry had said little about his visit when I saw him. I suspected that Gertie had roused his suspicions by talking so much about me, and by all the photographs about the room. And Perry might have heard gossip in the valley. Mission circles even in the city were small. In the country he could hardly have avoided the whispers had there been any. Now as the story of Gertie gushed into his ears, my detached self told me that its deductions were correct.

Another shower drove us to shelter in a golf course bunker. Perry held my hands in his, and we prayed together, for victory, consecration, strength, guidance, and courage to face temptation. I extracted one hand from Perry's to wipe my tears away. Then I promised earnestly and solemnly never again to allow the weakness of the flesh to mar my 'hope of glory'. My self-assurance, my conviction that I already had one foot in the 'field' lay shattered. However, now that the worst was known, and no more sin remained to be squeezed out of me, Perry's cheerfulness returned. He said he would make a new creation out of the bits. He would refashion me to be stronger than before. I was ready to believe anything at that moment. In Africa there would be no hot bodies with their unholy desires, but only our dedicated service to the teeming 'black folk'.

Exactly how Perry was to reconstruct my life of sanctity, was not clear, as he was going away from Belfast very soon. I dimly supposed he would pray for me, that letters would be written, and that we would be together possibly in the 'field'. When we got back from the woods, we went to the hall. And in the service was a hymn of consecration. I kept an eye on Perry as we sang it, for I wanted him to see my sincerity of purpose. He looked at me also, and was there, could it be, a slight suggestion of a wink? In the midst of the solemnity, such human reassurance was more comforting than divine promises. Immense happiness now replaced the afternoon wretchedness. Because somebody knew every dark deed and thought of my past, a great relief salved my wounded soul. Perry had been drawn closer to me. *There hath no temptation taken you*, he had quoted, *but such as is common to man*. Well, that was a comfort, anyway. Paradoxically, the moment of my highest happiness with Perry, was the one of deepest sadness, for it was our last time together. The following day, Monday, he would sail away from Ireland. and three months after, probably from Europe also. At the very least, years must pass before we would meet again, malarial, drum-tap, mud and straw compound, black-folk-healing, black-soul-saving years for him, but college-book and Bible, summer camp witness, learning-to-be-a-missionary years for me.

After the service, when Perry's hand was almost wrung from its wrist, a dozen or so of the congregation went off to Stanley's house. The Little Lady had prepared a fine farewell supper, although it was Sunday. But grace was said by so many of us, that the old woman had to rattle her ear-trumpet rather loudly as a signal to cut this short or else the eggs would get cold. Her large clock in a china case pinged ten o'clock before we rose from the table and the other guests departed. In that household, washing-up was always a time for the loudest possible chorus-singing. Stanley put on his apron and sang at the sink, working quickly enough to keep both Perry and I busy drying. The Little Lady put china into the glass-fronted cupboards, and laid cutlery in canteen boxes, lilting happily away to herself, at least one chorus behind the rest of us.

Claims of the chemist's shop meant that I would not see Perry on the Monday. Our farewell would be indeed under the Little Lady's roof. Under what palm-leaf thatch would we reunite in the years ahead? Perry took me then into the sitting-room, for a final bout of prayer. After his command of the situation during my golf course confession, Perry's nervousness at our imminent leave-taking surprised me. He faltered and failed to find words for the prayers. We stood up to say good-bye. Then, his hands took mine again. This time they did not let go. In some confusion I realized that Perry was trying to kiss me.

Perry let me go. Guilt possessed him then. It was worse than his previous nervousness. His displeasure worried me more than his pleasure. How could my bright sun become cloudy so quickly, the cheerfulness descend to brooding melancholy? The meteoric fall from being Perry's special friend to being the cause of his remorse, upset me bitterly. I could not go home until we made it up. In a kind of panic, I could not bear to think of all the years ahead when Perry would be carrying resentment against me. But Perry rejected me. I could not understand his volatile moods.

Then Perry cut me to the core. 'You are such a child really,' he said, and buried his head in his hands by the fire.

I asked him desperately when he was going to speak to his principal about my training. He did not look at me, or give an answer. When at last he spoke, it was on a new subject, at least new to him, but not to me. 'You must wait,' he said.

Again I was told to learn to walk, before running madly into something of such importance. He sounded just as pompous as everyone else who had said I must wait. How could Perry fail to understand my burning desire to get on with my life as a missionary—after all, he must have experienced it himself. But he went on with his nauseating platitudes, until I could bear it no longer. It was as if he had slammed the door of his real self in my face. All I could see of him was a dead puppet, moving like a preacher, a mask hiding the real Perry, whom it appeared I had lost now for ever. What happened while we were saying good-bye had not meant anything to me. I did not resent Perry because of it. It had been rather a sloppy, impulsive incident to me. But it had changed my friend into a poker-faced platitude-monger.

Spring Fervour

Quite plainly he wanted me to clear out of the house before my loud talking brought Stanley to the room.

Because he spurned my offer of friendship, it happened. Primitive instincts rose in me. I forgot about being 'saved', and that I was grown-up now, and that I was almost a missionary. Somehow I had to penetrate Perry's armour of indifference. If friendliness would not do so, then enmity should. Resorting to the old urges of children fighting in the entry, I flung wicked abuse at Perry, and dared him with my fists. We were out in the hall now. At one side stood a standard jardinière shaped like a tree trunk with bears climbing the branch stumps. I sent the whole thing crashing at Perry's feet and dashed out of the house, mixed tears of anger and sorrow blinding me.

Hurrying along the streets I schemed ways of hurting Perry. First I would break all the promises I had made to him in the golf bunker. I would deliberately break the next Sabbath both by travelling and in going to see Gertie—my Gertie.

CHAPTER XII

A Whiff of Incense

In the deserted streets I succumbed to the old city-by-night spell. As far back as I could remember it had always been there. At the end of the day, you always came back to the tramless roads, the litter-strewn pavements. If you had run out of the house in anger earlier in the day, it was through these eerie chasms of brick that you crept home repentant. And if you had been up with the sun, and out to the woods, or along the wader coasts, or looking for eggs in the bog-cotton moors, they were always waiting to close you in again, the blank windows, the bolted doors, the shuttered shops. Before you were grown-up, this was almost the only time when you seemed to belong to the city. Silence lay like snow, covering indiscriminately, levelling entry and grand lime-lined avenue to the same pale ghostliness. By night, the solid city became insubstantial. Living people boxed behind its walls became unreal. Those who lived there in former days seemed to peer with dead faces from the rooms you hurried past. Down alleyways, you almost saw the shadow of skipping-ropes still turning for long-dead children. But you never heard voices, the squeals of laughter, the last call of the children to bed. Silence covered all that.

When nobody wanted you, the nocturnal streets accepted

you. They could hide you anonymously in the queer, angled light of street-lamps. The black-out, when it came, did not make much difference. Secrecy became all the greater. And chinks of light always escaped, over fanlights or between carelessly drawn curtains.

Nowhere had haunted me more than the warehouse area downtown. Few memories came before that. Huge horses had always stood in the courtyard archways. They looked down at me, mysteriously gas-masked with nosebags. When I was very tiny, my mother had tried to get through an archway, squeezing in the narrow space left by the shafts. As I followed, timorously avoiding the hooves, up went the nosebag showering me with a delicious snow of chopped hay. Tickled perhaps by the small figure creeping by, the horse smote a hoof on the granite setts, striking a light like a flint. I realized that one blow from those shaggy hooves would kill me. But Big 'Ina was not afraid. She patted the shiny horse and lifted me up to do the same. Afterwards I went alone to the warehouses, passing every archway where the patient animals stood.

Going away to Fermanagh did not kill my childhood pleasure. Most of the horses had gone by the time I came back to Belfast. Motor-vans dripped grease where the oats and hay had been sprinkled. But the warehouses remained, fabulous castles to me, grim and powerful. 'Conversion' had caused grave doubts as to whether a 'Christian' should prowl about so late at night. But I had taken the long way home nevertheless, even after the devoutest prayer session.

So I hurried to the warehouses now, with Perry's dreadful words still caustic in my ears. Close to the dark walls, I could lose myself, take comfort from the thick fortresses, gulp draughts of calmness from their solitude. When I thought of childhood and sparkling, ringing hooves clopping in and out with loaded wagons, Perry and his like did not matter so much. They had not penetrated my life as deeply as the memories. For years I had known the most fascinating route through the labyrinth of streets, and as I followed it again my distress at Perry's treachery began to subside.

'Hi!'

A voice from a deep doorway in a business street startled me. I stopped, peering into the dim recess. Two faces appeared when a cigarette glowed.

'What's the hurry?' asked another voice.

None. There was none. No hurry at all. I had finished with Perry, with the mission hall, with all of it. Therefore I had all the time in the world. I took the cigarette offered by one of the American soldiers and sat with them on the top step. There were always people. Somewhere. Perry can't turn me out, I thought. Nobody can. The world isn't a desert. There's always an oasis.

The Americans had spent their evening on the booze (my first instinct had been to hand them a tract for drunks which showed a man drowning in a sea labelled DRINK). Now they sat on some goddam steps, they didn't know where. They were more than normally conscious of being alone. So you are, in this universe. But you can disguise the being alone. When my first cigarette spun towards the gutter like a meteorite, they gave me another, and a bottle. The fiery spirit ran inside my throat, flushing my whole body with warmth. I never had such a sensation before. Not even on cold nights aboard the reclaimer.

'It's O.K.,' I said.

They wanted me to like it. The drink's taste was vile, but made me feel warm. I told them so and they laughed, pleased to give hospitality, even if it was only on a doorstep. Squatting there in the clear, starry night, drinking with a couple of strangers, was just the antidote I needed to months of tee-total cant at mission halls. In rich drawls they told me all about exotic places, North Carolina and Arizona. I could well understand now the irresistible Yankee charm to which my sister succumbed. They didn't care a damn for anybody, for anything. Out came the photographs. We held lighters to look at home and mom. And the girls. That set us off. Sexy talk about big breasts and legs. I was secretly astonished at the numbers of girls the G.I.s knew. They remembered the minutest detail, besides the way they walked or sat with tight, low-cut dresses at drug-store counters. What a relief it was for me to join in their swearing and blasphemies. I wished Perry was there to hear me, just to shock his self-righteous ears. Foul language meant nothing to me. Too many years as a child had been spent to the accompaniment of a spicy vocabulary. But what a two-edged sword in Perry's soul my bad words would be! How I wished the wind, which sprang into our doorway now and again, would bear the terrible words, and blow them at that precious prig.

Quite suddenly, I felt cold, and the stone steps struck chill on my legs. The bottle was empty, and one of the soldiers had fallen asleep in the corner. It was late and I wanted my bed. Walking home I grew flushed again. The sharp air sent the whisky into my head. In bed, a loose happiness seized me. A slight rocking motion, like being on a dredger again, sent me to sleep. But I woke freezing, in the desolate pre-dawn. The comfort lent by the doorway incident seemed a foolish thing. And I had fallen into bed without saying my prayers. Though I had pushed aside mission halls, my belief in God and His wrath to come could not be treated in that way. I got out of bed, and put my trousers on to address my Maker. I had not yet been introduced to pyjamas and thought that my nudity would shock the Almighty. Instinctively I said *Our*

Father and the Church Lads' Brigade prayer. These had been my litany for years, until the night I was 'born again' and forsook formal prayers.

That night I slept little and got up for work feeling wretched. What could I fill my week with, now that my happy, busy life had vanished overnight? At the chemists I fumbled about and dropped things. I could not get Perry out of my mind. A hundred times I looked at my watch to see if it was time for his boat to sail. Six o'clock closing could not come quickly enough. I already knew where I would go when it did. My fire-watching duty fell on Monday nights. Usually, I went out to tea with Stanley. But that night I would go to a pub. All my life I had been in and out of pubs, and knew them almost as well as churches and meeting halls. But that had only been to take the empties for my mother's boy-friends. But my own manhood could be proved now.

Around the docks area, nobody would recognize me, and I was quite confident of not being detected as under age. I asked for porter. Men with 'porter bellies' were supposed to be strong and virile. I wanted to be like that. After knocking it back, I got a second, and began to feel better. I noticed how the noise in the bar came up, wrapping me like a warm coat. People seemed to talk quicker and louder than outside. They laughed a lot and simple remarks scintillated like real wit. And the lights too had a harder glitter. In the elaborate cut-glass, bare bulbs were multiplied until the whole bar sparkled like a coruscating chandelier. The comfort was prenatal, womb-like. Tobacco haze, mahogany bars and seats, matured barrels, lincrusta walls and ceiling, held me in a bosom embrace, and suckled me tenderly. In this fuzzy, undersea world, outlines vanished. Like a marine animal that neither walks nor swims, the barman hovered ready to feed me with more drink. I wished he would either float away or else talk directly with me. But his eyes looked at me like a crab's, gristly and depthless.

From my experiences aboard the reclaimer, I was aware, in spite of my haziness, of how insignificant a couple of pints were. A really big 'wet' meant ten pints at the very least. Yet I was bursting already. Well, the remedy for that was at the back of the pub, in the yard. Soon I was running back and forth to the lavatory, a little surprised to see grown men making the highest possible parabolas with their water, just as we used to do when children.

From the dark yard I plunged into the yellow warmth again, where voices surged like lazy tides. More porter. More people talked to me, not caring whether I listened or not, but anxious for my laughter. I could imagine them wanting my tears too, if the mood demanded. Anything would do, as long as they had communion. Anything to stop being alone, like the two G.I.s the night before. How surprisingly ordinary the people were, not stiff in a corset of salvation. But they were unique too, the walrus-moustached dockers, that big blousy woman with the hoarse hearty laugh, the bemused Tommies sweating over pint races, the pathetic procession of old crones poking bottoms to clear the way for ewers of porter concealed beneath their black shawls. Beyond the immediate circle that hemmed me in, a less distinct crush existed, grass-widows, fruity sailors, all smoking or snuffing, hoping or despairing, all blessed or cursed with wet feet, sexy eyes, smelly bodies, running noses.

Then like a showman folding his puppets away, collapsing his ramshackle theatre, the barman shouted time and winked the lights on and off. As reluctantly as dissolving snows, the pub crowd melted away. How terrible, I thought, for this fine world to crumble so suddenly, become nothing at the mere striking of a clock. Not wanting to be responsible for destroying the evening's happiness, people began to leave unobtrusively, but in pairs or groups. They would carry away with them a little of the tinsel brilliance. There might be bottles at home too. But not for me. The cold street waited outside and I must walk it alone. The idea of facing an empty bed did not help my fit of depression.

The novelty of tilted pavements, leaning walls, gyrating street-lamps created a comic situation when I got outside. I must have been one of the last, for I heard the barman bolting the door behind me. On starting to walk I discovered that the normal laws of gravity were temporarily suspended. Sometimes my body leaned dangerously towards the ground, pulled there by a strong force. Then in the next moment, a bout of levitation carried me off. And just as I got used to the blissful floating, my limbs would turn to lead, and the gutter reared up again. Bed did not appear a bad place after all. I fought my way to the draper's where I was to fire-watch.

Pausing from their game, the card-players gave me an odd look when I passed through to the bedroom. Nobody had bothered to light the gas-fire. It resisted my fumblings, hissed and popped protestingly, but finally capitulated. Its glare struck pleasantly on my face as I turned it full on. With a gesture of abandonment I threw myself back on the bed. Up it came, almost tipping me on the floor. Then it spun like a roulette wheel, then it hinged in the opposite direction, then it rocked like a bumboat. In a foul, bilious heaving, my stomach threw up. Could degradation plumb lower depths? Even after being sick, the giddiness continued. Never could I remember such wretchedness. Not only did I feel terribly ill but not a shred of self-respect was left. Was this wreck Maggie's Cub, Big 'Ina's 'wee fella', the zealous 'soul-winner', the invincible missionary? I wanted to die.

And I almost did too, because the blankets caught fire.

Luckily for me the card-players smelt burning, rushed in, and stripped off the smoking bedclothes. Certainly in that drunken, heavy sleep I should not have felt the smouldering which a kicked-off blanket and the unguarded gas-fire had caused. With a minimum of fuss and words, the figures moved about the room, washed and cleaned me up, put my shirt on me, and carried me like a sack of potatoes to an adjacent bed. Making sure there was no other danger from naked gas flames, they closed the door and returned to the poker-table. What must they think now of their hot-gospeller?

Early in the morning, somebody brought me a cup of tea. I gulped it gratefully. A door far away down, slammed. I realized the garret was empty now. In the permanently blacked-out room contrition walked hand in hand with affliction. As the tea went down, warming and strengthening, I saw, quite clearly, the hand of God in the night's events. *The Lord will destroy the house of the proud.* Being too cocksure had brought it all on me. God, I thought, could teach me by no means other than to bring me low in my own estimation. Wise, good, clever, sweet God, He had plucked me, literally, as a brand from another kind of burning, and I gave humble thanks for deliverance. If only my head would clear, and the nausea go, I would get out my Scripture Union notes again. 'Backsliding' and the 'world' would never again hold any attraction.

At the shop, Billy gave me some tablets which helped to remedy the night's damage. By the forenoon the biliousness had gone and the wedge splitting my head open had been extracted. For good measure he gave me a second dose and packed me off down town for a wholesale order. The supplies took an hour to organize, so I had some free time to wander the streets. My 'Jesus Saves' badge was back in place. A squally shower from the Lough sent me scuttling to St. George's Church for shelter. At first I stood amongst the great pillars of the front looking out at the suddenly-shiny street. Although rain beat against the walls, it was curiosity that finally drove me inside the building. My elder sister had taken me when I was a child. She held my hand lest I should run about and cause disturbance. But there was no need. Wide-eyed with wonder, I peered into the dark roof, trying to comprehend infinity. And from the chancel, pure springs of music had sent out trickles that joined to a mighty river invisible over my head. That the men and boys dressed up pleased me immensely, surplices lent the singing a dignity quite distinct from the other city choirs. Later on people had marred my regard for St. George's by labelling it 'high' and therefore not for me. After getting 'saved', of course, St. George's was one of the places where I went with my tracts. Left on the pews, these strongly worded warnings would be picked up by the 'unsaved' as they went about their Romish bowing and scraping. Now in the rain I was more interested in what was going on than in distributing Gospel tracts.

Holy Communion was being celebrated.

From the shadows a verger emerged and showed me to a place near the front. I had only intended to escape the rain and do my good deed, now I was involved in the service. It made me nervous, for since my confirmation in Fermanagh two years previously, I had not taken my first communion. And though on most Sundays I had partaken of the breaking-of-bread in mission halls, atmosphere was utterly lacking. On several occasions I had myself blessed farmhouse loaves, and torn them asunder for the round-the-kitchen-table conventicle communion. How distressed it made me after one service, to see remains of the blessed bread thrown to the chickens. As the figures moved quietly about St. George's altar, the solemnity of those holy mysteries seemed like a pool where I could bathe away the heat and sweat of sin. Because I had left the mission hall prejudices outside in the rain, the communicants' humility seemed beautiful. With what simple penitence they sank to their knees to receive the sacrament. How much finer a way this was to honour a forgiving God. In conventicles we lounged on our benches, cross-kneed or bolt upright, while the bread-plate went round, and the loaf was fingered as though we were ravenous with physical rather than spiritual hunger. What better reparation for the vile night could I make than to take my first communion? Both breaches would be healed at once, that between God and myself, and that between my drunken lapse and the happy person I had been in Fermanagh. Concealing excitement, I went to the rail.

Within a month I was completely at home in St. George's. Crossing myself, genuflecting and other ritualistic behaviour came easily to me despite life-long Protestant indoctrination. Intoning seemed the most natural way to express liturgy. The attraction was that God's services no longer depended precariously on the individual. By drastic means I had learnt the dangers of relying on your own powers. When you went down, nothing but ruins remained. St. George's went in for more serious activities than Tract Bands. The Rector introduced me to a class of late vocations doing Latin and Greek. For evangelicals, I had been too young, but now it appeared I was behindhand, and must catch up with my studies. And to be a missionary still stood as my principal aim, though first I must be ordained. Anglican-minded clergy other than those at St. George's became interested in me, and helped with coaching me or lending books. One of them wrote to an English college which took younger candidates, whom they first prepared for matriculation. So I heard of Kelham.

Naturally, I did not mention the proper name of this to my mother, or anyone at home. They would never have believed that *The Society of the Sacred Mission* was Protestant. But nobody would stop me from going. My mother knew well enough by this time that I was profoundly serious about 'the Call'. Also, she realized it meant, at last, the death knell of her old dream for me, that I should undertake a shipyard apprenticeship. The dream castle she had struggled so long to capture for me and my future, finally dissolved into thin air. Yet because I had turned out to be 'good living', despite years of evidence to the contrary, I was bound to do everything all right. A pang or two must have caused her worry when she realized my sixteenth birthday was due. That date had been fixed, at one time, for the beginning of my engineering training. Now it would come and go, and I would be like the numbers in our family who had no trade. Yet she regarded my plan of being a missionary with the best possible grace. Perhaps she felt so grateful to God for keeping me out of 'trouble' for so long, that she was prepared to let Him do anything He pleased with me. This made things easier at home for me.

References from other clergy who had known me for some time, were required to support the Kelham application. But only one cleric in the Church of Ireland really knew me, our own Rector, Ould Willie. Here was a difficulty. How could I dare to approach him, after flinging away the wonderful opening in naval training he made for me? For a year now I had always avoided him in the street, fearful he would reproach my thoughtless selfishness. Whenever I saw him coming, threading his way through the crowds, I had dashed into entries. He must have been fully aware of how I constantly and blatantly evaded him. And however brave I might be at a street-corner witness service surrounded by mockers, I could not face Ould Willie. Evangelical duty had demanded that I confront him and ask whether he was a 'born again Christian' or not, but courage failed. Evasion, however, was no longer possible. Ould Willie alone could testify to my upbringing and church background.

Heart once more in mouth, I went to the rectory. But again my fears were groundless. Without a word about the navy, or the Irish Guards, without a question as to where I worshipped, Ould Willie scanned my Kelham application. He knew all about Anglo-Catholicism, and as a well-known figure in the Orange Order, did not approve of it. We sat by his study fire, he on one side, I on the other. While he read, I looked round the room I knew so well. Every Saturday for seven years I had come to it for the orphanage money which supported us. I knew every photograph of university teams, of clerical groups, of venerable men in his life, and the one on the desk, showing his wife. She looked young and was wearing a comic dress of many years earlier. The pattern of reference books behind the glass doors was almost as familiar as the old wallpaper had been in my own bedroom. Long ago I had learnt by heart the few texts filling up odd places between bookcases and pictures. None of it had changed. How many hundreds of signatures had I signed at the desk, as the Rector handed over the precious fifteen shillings?

There could be few who knew human frailty like Ould Willie. There was certainly nobody who knew mine so well, my every weakness, my first dangers, my last escapades, my penitent's tears, the inevitable recidivism. As I asked him to recommend me for training as a priest, did he remember the path behind me, strewn with misdemeanours? Did he recall that his own sexton had found me plundering the poor box? As I explained my missionary ambition, I hoped Ould Willie would not think of poor Miss Greyfell's missionary box which I had robbed to buy roller-skates. His parish embraced many bad streets, but it was doubtful if any boy ever gave him such trouble and anxiety as I had. To me Ould Willie had been much more than a 'father in God'. Though I grew quickly from a child into a lanky boy he had always known my size in clothes and shoes, and kept his eyes open at jumble sales. That I left home as an evacuee instead of going to a remand home was principally his doing. In a room over the study Ould Willie's son was practising the piano, the son who years before had come specially to sit by me in church. It was the Sunday morning after my 'visits' to Miss Greyfell's came to light, and he made me promise, for my own sake, never to go house-breaking again. In that room, so redolent of things bygone, where past and present mingled like a rich solera, Ould Willie could hardly forget the hard years. Yet he apparently remembered nothing, only that I was still his parish orphan and in need of support. He would withhold nothing.

Off went the application. There could be no obstacle now. Instead of being a burning point high overhead, beyond reach, my African sun suddenly loomed low and fiery on the horizon. I thought of it as a ripe fruit, for which I had only to stretch out a hand and pluck. Then came word Godspeed from England. Kelham could not finally admit me without a personal interview. This was a blow. Travel between Ulster and England required a permit in the form of a paper-backed passport, made valid for each crossing. But the same week that I applied for a permit, all travel across The Water was completely banned, except for troops. We did not know then, but D.Day was near. I was frustrated but went on with my Greek and boiling carrageen moss.

Going home from the chemist's one evening, I collided

with Stanley in the tram. Though he must have heard my quarrel with Perry in the hall, he showed his usual friendliness. He was intrigued when I said that my training would soon begin. But wickedly, I wanted to shock him, and opened a book that mentioned Kelham. It also had a photograph of the famous rood. Horror-struck, Stanley could think of nothing to say, and parted with a promise to pray for my 'backsliding'. Baiting this gentle person caused me not a little amusement. I knew how staunchly Protestant he was, how susceptible to attack. In their sitting-room at home, a 'young people's squash meeting' had been held, and I had asked if we might sing 'Lead kindly light'. Not only was anything by Cardinal Newman proscribed, but the large hymnal on the piano had been 'purified' by having the hymn cut out.

A telephone call at the chemist's interrupted my work next morning. I heard the Little Lady's voice at the other end. Obviously, I could not shout the shop down to make her hear. But she had no wish to hear me. In fact she had telephoned herself in preference to Stanley, in order that this might be so. The Little Lady's soul burned within her, as she warned me about selling my 'precious soul for a whiff of incense'. Her voice quavered with kindness and concern. Would I go to supper with them. My acceptance must have been presumed, for she could not hear my 'Yes'.

A hand clutched the dancing lace cherub on the curtains—the Little Lady's. She kept her usual watch by the window to see me arrive. While I walked up the garden path, I knew she would be hopping among the footstools on her way to open the door. Everything in the furniture-cluttered house remained as before. Nobody had eaten the succulent wax fruit under its cloche, the wax roses on the table showed no sign of dropping their petals. And the Little Lady did not mention the night I had stormed out, rattling the panes of coloured

glass in the front door when I slammed it. She merely made a
kind enquiry as to whether I had hurt myself when I fell in
the hallway. We did not waste words on niceties.

Perry was never mentioned in that house again. Except by
Stanley, who hoped that I had not heard from Perry, who
had proved not to be 'sound'. During the war certain
evangelicals believed Hitler to be Antichrist, and therefore
bound to win. After leaving Belfast, Perry's plans for going
to Africa were upset by war circumstances. This led him into
the Hitler-Antichrist camp. By extremely suspect methods,
these people applied mathematics to a verse from *The Book
of Revelation.* Antichrist, said the verse, was a man with the
number 'Six hundred threescore and six'. They prepared
elaborate diagrams containing dates of Hitler's birth, subse-
quent career, and similar nonsense. Then by an abstruse process they manipulated the figures and as an answer got 666!
Even at Easter, several eyebrows had been raised disapprov-
ingly at Perry's views on prophesy. And now word reached
the hall, that not only did Perry believe this, but had been in
conflict with the authorities for preaching about the Hitler-
Antichrist winning the war. This caused a grave scandal, for,
though 'saved', the people at the mission hall were highly
patriotic Britishers.

Stanley had taken my Kelham application with serious
concern. Already two prayer-meetings had been held about
it. But long experience had taught the Little Lady that such
matters brook no delay, and so she produced a concrete plan.
Since I was determined to stay within the Church of Ireland,
why did I not join up with some of the evangelical parishes,
rather than with its popery? This would even mean that I
could go to one of the interdenominational training colleges.
At this I pricked up my ears. I was getting rather weary with
claims and counter-claims from the multitude of dissenting

sects. Each maintained that it, and none other, was the reposi-
tory of truth. I was tempted to stop my ears up. But the
possibility of entering quickly into a college revived my flag-
ging interest. Because of approaching D-Day, my Kelham
application lay dormant. I would willingly sacrifice it for
immediate action elsewhere. Anything to get my training
over, and out to Africa. The Little Lady brought out her
trump card then, a magazine with the names of several
colleges, and her promise of financial support. Their courses
took only a fraction of the time which Kelham needed. For
me this was a criterion, and I agreed to write for a prospectus.

The booklet and forms came by return post, practically
bursting out of the envelope with enthusiasm. Without too
much hope, I filled in the papers and sent them back. The out-
come would probably not be encouraging, as I had plainly
stated two things to disadvantage, my age, and high church
connection. But an even speedier answer came. They
accepted me! No delay, no personal interview. I only needed
permission to travel. And that was not all. My first term's
fees had already been paid and the second term's promised,
both with a generous margin for pocket money. The Lord
had opened the heart and purse of some dear old English
woman, when she heard my case prayed for in the college
prayer-meeting. Nobody, however, felt that they should
point out to me that the college suffered from a dearth of
candidates, that it was saved from government requisition
only because it was occupied by a few conscientious objectors,
cripples, and medical dischargees from the Forces. Young I
might be, but at least I was old enough to fill another bed and
help to keep those wolves from the door—the evacuees.

Overjoyed, I ran all the way to Stanley's house, and spread
the letter before the Little Lady. *Jehovah-jireh*, what praises
did she not shout, while she lifted her skirt and filled my hand

233

with bank-notes. She must be the first to pay my fare to England—a little jealous perhaps of the unknown English 'sister' who had forestalled her with the fees. No thought of work could be entertained that morning and I went straight to the permit office. But I met impassive faces, barred doors. The ban on travelling was even more stringent than previously and no one, no matter of what importance, could cross to or from England. The island's separation was complete. Crestfallen I returned to the Little Lady. But she merely tut-tutted, and sucked her cheeks at all the generals and ministers, the civil servants and port authorities who stood in our way. The Lord, she said, had vanquished kings before now. The North Channel would divide before me as the Red Sea had divided for Moses.

My contacts in high places were non-existent, but not the Little Lady's. While I sat near the window, silent with disappointment, she began a letter, making precise scratches across the page in her old-fashioned copperplate hand. Although I could not begin my actual studies until September, and now it was only May, urgency was real nevertheless. Fearful lest a delay should allow second thoughts about Anglo-Catholicism, the training college wanted me to leave immediately. They had planned for me to spend the summer months in England, on a student campaign on the holiday beaches. Amongst the 'ungodly' there, I would be too busy evangelizing and getting used to English ways, to bother any more about whiffs of incense. I posted the Little Lady's letter. The envelope bore the name of a prominent lawyer, who besides being a highly influential man, was a real 'born again Christian'. Indeed, one of his colleagues had gone off to help found the African mission which I hoped to join. However, the suspension of journeys out of Northern Ireland applied equally to exalted people, and for the moment, even the lawyer's good offices could procure nothing. Moses himself, it seemed, would have been refused access to the sea.

At major crises in my life, I seemed to fly away to Fermanagh. The lakes and green hills always restored me. And I flew there again now, to await any easing in the travel ban. The lawyer had promised that at the first opportunity he would push my case forward. As the train rushed me westwards once again, I found that my excited nerves did not quieten as they usually did. I turned up at Maggie's farm in the same state of tension as I left Belfast. Here at any rate, I could prepare to leave Ireland.

Work on the farm was in full swing, but I could not settle to it. The peaceful rhythm of its long days, was out of time with the pace of my thoughts. Early summer days that once had been too short between the sun's rising and setting, now became too long. Ages seemed to pass between the clearing of the morning dew till Maggie blew the whistle for dinner. I seemed to go through a whole lifetime between our watering of the calves and the evening milking. The songs and round-the-fire stories of the evening *ceilis* seemed pointless while my fate hung in the balance. In the fields I waited anxiously to hear the creamery lorry return after twelve. Then whatever was doing, I would drop it and run over to the next farm in time to hear the one o'clock news, for Maggie had no wireless. And in the late afternoons I cycled into Enniskillen to pick up the Belfast papers. I was afraid that something would go wrong at the last minute, or that the ban would be lifted without my knowing.

Maggie suffered with me, my anguish became hers. But she tackled it in a practical way and devised schemes to keep me occupied. Enough things needed organizing without my wasting time waiting for the postman or the girl from the Post Office to bring me a telegram. Maggie let me have the whole blackcurrant crop from the gardens to sell. The money helped to buy some of the clothes set out on the college list. Maggie took charge of things, insisting that only the best would do. Each day, our fingers ran further down the column. When they got to 'table napkins' out came some three-feet squares of fine linen that were bought at the sale of an old abbey. The pyjamas caused a disturbance in my normal way of life. I had to train myself to dress up in them. For the first few nights, after the curious striped garments had been bought in town, my limbs felt as if they were fettered. But I acknowledged them as an indispensable aid to a life of sanctity. Indeed, from the day when the college accepted me I had been going about in such a state of holiness that I dared not think of my own body or anyone else's, let alone look at them. Poor Gertie's letters still arrived with an embarrassing frequency, but I burnt them unread. Such things as they contained might easily displease the Lord. I dare not risk His stopping my travel permit.

Christy trundled into town some days on his rusty old bike and brought the newspapers back. On that particular Monday he handed them to me as I worked amongst the currant bushes. With purple-stained fingers I held a paper up and saw the thick black headline, BAN LIFTED FOR DIPLO-MATS.

'Lifted,' I shouted, running into the house. 'The ban's lifted.'

Diplomats, whoever they might be, were now allowed across The Water to the wonderland of England. Somebody at least was going, but who exactly were these strange people, 'diplomats'? I did not know, neither did Maggie, except, of course, that they were bigwigs. To speed her churning she put hot water in and dashed it off quickly. When the butter was washed we went into the kitchen. Maggie stood on a stool to get down the old dictionary that propped up the cuckoo clock on the dresser. 'To invest with a privilege' it said for diplomat. Yes that was me. One of the greatest privileges in the 'Christian' life people always told me, was to be given 'the Call', and I had that I was certain. And as to 'transacting business for a sovereign at a foreign court', I was better than that. Maggie had to agree that as a messenger of the King of Kings to 'foreign parts', I must be included in the group for whom the ban was lifted.

With such vital news in the house, I could not even wait until next morning. My new clothes were ready. We just had time to get the ass cart out and rush into Enniskillen to catch the last train back to Belfast.

CHAPTER XIII

Perfect Cadence

When the train steamed into Belfast, my nerves were shredded. I thought I could hardly survive until morning. I got up early and went to the Little Lady's house to let her know developments. She had not been idle since the news broke. During the night she had spent a long prayer session 'at the Throne' and assured me of her conviction that the Lord was at work. He must have been, for later, the lawyer friend went to the permit office. Before the Little Lady sat down to her luncheon, a telephone message came through. I was to present myself to the officials again. Stanley took a half day off work and came with me. While I went into an inner office, he remained outside, praying that I might be 'guided' to say the right thing. Inside, an important-looking government man fingered files and top copies, and took a great deal of circumambulation to come to the point. My nervous agitation, my missionary zeal, seemed to move him not at all. He wrote things on papers, and then it was over. I came out feeling that his promise of writing to me within twenty-four hours, was a polite way to get rid of me. Stanley, on the other hand, was quite certain he had 'got through' with his prayers.

The mission hall elders insisted that our spiritual power

depended solely on the length of time we spent praying.
John Wesley had been so busy that he found it necessary to
have four hours daily 'at the Throne'. I found even two exhausting. But Stanley, despite his puny physique and shyness,
was such a spiritual lion. We were to have now an all-night
session of prayer! If the granting of my travel permit was
guaranteed by such a marathon, then I was all for it. As I
went home to my mother's for tea, and to prepare myself for
the nocturnal session, Satan cast doubts in my mind—as if
prayer *really* made any difference, as if *they* would give *me* a
permit, as if God was not too busy in any case to bother with
such minutiae. And what a fool I would look when the praying was over but the permit refused.

My nerves were so on edge that the noise at home was un-
bearable. The crashing and clanking of trains and trams, the
gabble of lodgers home from work, Big 'Ina's high spirits, all
tore at my peace of mind. More than anything I wanted
quietude, so I left the house and walked out to the swampy
steppes of the Bog Meadows. And there I saw Aggie Moore
out exercising her greyhound, wandering about the sad
open stretches, like a ghost. So she was in a way, a ghost from
my early life in the city, when the Bog Meadows was all I
knew of the countryside. How strange, I thought, that Aggie
Moore and her dog should appear on what might prove to
be one of my last nights in Ireland. So many scenes came to
me as I watched her. Only a few years before, I had deemed
it a great privilege to be allowed to take Sal, her greyhound,
out to the Bog Meadows. Now Aggie had grown so old that
she had given up her second-hand clothes-shop. But her fame
as a fortune-teller lived on undimmed.

A little wind was playing about the grass and the tinkers'
rag-tents. I could not tell whether it came from the mountains or the Lough. But it brought with it the voice of the

Evil One. A reading with Aggie, came the voice, would reveal my future, show all my plans. Aggie Moore was a sweet old soul, and remembered well enough how I had roamed the Meadows with Sal. But as she chatted about what a fine young man I was, so different from the pale thin boy who had called for her Sal, I was praying 'Lord give me the victory, Lord give me the victory'. Rather abruptly I bid Aggie Moore good-bye and went farther over the waste lands. Wrestle as I might with my conscience, there could be no denying that Aggie's forecast of my future *would* relieve the tension inside me. If I did not know something definite soon, surely my head must burst. Jumping the meandering streams, as I had jumped them long ago when catching spricks with the tinker children, did not soothe me. The permit worried me so much, I did not even pause to wonder where those dark, wild children might be, now that they had grown to be sixteen like myself.

In an off-guarded moment, when I was not actually praying, I turned and ran madly back to try and catch up with Aggie Moore. But she had gone home, so once again I was saved from dabbling with evil. I passed her house, walked bravely to the end of her street. At the corner I paused, and then went back again. After doing this twice, I could bear suspense no more, and knocked at her door. A few moments must elapse before she could answer. There was still time to come out on the Lord's side, but I stood rooted, waiting for the bolt of the door to be unfastened. Aggie expressed herself only too pleased to do my hands and the crystal. We had not to plunge into the occult very deeply before she made a significant remark. The rest could not interest me. Aggie said quite plainly that I was about to go on a journey which would mean crossing water.

I left her hastily as before, now wanting to whoop with

joy. Aggie Moore had certainly played the role of angel rather than old witch. There was no one to whom I could tell the good news, certainly not Stanley or the Little Lady. Thoughts of how horrified they would be at my reverting to the black arts, sent me out to the Bog Meadows again to pray for my 'backsliding'. But Aggie's reading had given me great relief. From the earliest years, I heard of her powerful ability. Peering into the future had always been a failing of mine. One of my first questions at every new Fermanagh billet as an evacuee, had been to ask if anyone around read tea-cups. Even after 'conversion' I found it difficult to sit in the house and not pick up a 'worldly' newspaper and hunt out my horoscope. The message of the stars and of tea-leaves had once been such a comfort. Its fascination survived my 'second birth'. But indulgence demanded repentance and forgiveness. I prayed for them out in the Bog Meadows. On my way to the prayer-meeting at Stanley's, I popped a tract into Aggie Moore's letter-box.

Afterwards it was difficult to recall how the night hours passed in the Little Lady's sitting-room. Looking back, they took no form or pattern, but stretched through the darkest hours, like the earth, void before creation. Six of us kept the vigil, though I had to be poked occasionally to be kept awake. Dandelion coffee and a plentiful supply of black-market biscuits broke the monotony and saved us from physical tiredness. But from where the others found enough things to pray aloud was really puzzling. At last a kind of dawn broke and the sky turned from dark serge to grey flannel—there was certainly no beauty in it for me after those gruelling hours. Looking decidedly pouchy about the eyes the others went off to their beds. Another *crise de nerfs* sent me flying home to await the post, though hours must pass before first delivery.

Daylight grew stronger. I could see everything clearly in

our kitchen as I began praying again. My prayers were desperate ones now, filled with the same fervour and intentness as when I begged for my hump to be taken away. The lodgers came down to breakfast, surprised to find me there so early, so I went out and continued praying in the lavatory. At last everyone had gone to work and the house was mine again. Urgency poured into my prayers and I uttered them aloud. At every breath I paused, listening for the postman's footsteps. Trains went by at the back, a milk van at the front, and I could hear the woman next door call her children to get up, as clearly as if in our own house. Then at last, several doors away I heard the rat-a-tat and the metallic click of letter-box flaps. He was coming! I knelt in the hall now, the lino cold against my knees. Praying. Praying. Praying. Yet I could not dismiss Aggie Moore's prophesy. Clump, clump came the postman's boots. My body threatened to collapse as they stopped at our door. Something fluttered gently to the door-mat. I opened my eyes and looked.

It was only a postcard.

Surely my heart must now break in bitter disappointment. But no, the brass flap opened again and the permit fell to the floor with the soft, silken sound of falling manna. Of course, I had known it *would* come, but my life had been full of certain things that somehow, at the last minute, failed me. Anyway, the priceless document was mine now, key to a continent. Immediate, but slow relaxation set in. I booked a ticket on the boat, telephoned the tidings to Stanley, and went home to sleep. Days of tension, and hours without sleep, laid me flat like a knocked-out prize-fighter. Not until that evening did I realize the extent of my boorish ingratitude to the Lord. While I had been sleeping, eating, and dreaming of far-away places, the faithful had been offering all sorts of thanks throughout the day. Indeed, my first impulse on getting the permit had been to rush round to Aggie Moore's and give her another half-crown. Her reading seemed so much more directly responsible than all the prayers and supplication of the brethren. And as a celebration I had even allowed myself to think of Gertie and sent her a letter—a spiritual message only, informing her of victory in answer to prayer, and the voyage arrangements. At the last service in the mission hall I delivered a farewell message. It must have been rousing enough, for the next morning's post brought a number of anonymous letters, all containing money to speed me on the first stage to Africa.

For all the accommodation available, the North Channel might have been as wide as the Atlantic. Only one boat could squeeze me in and that was the steamer plying between Larne and Stranraer. It sailed two days following the arrival of my permit. Hardly soon enough! I was ready. Although my trunk was not so imposing as the one we gave Perry, at least it bore the curious label of an Egyptian hotel, proof enough that tropical suns had already baked its great iron corners and camphor-smelling inside. In addition to this *pièce de résistance* two portmanteaux made up the luggage, and they were still as perfect as the day when the Little Lady had first used them when travelling to the Keswick Convention.

I said good-bye to my mother before she left for her shift. We did not look at each other. At moments of emotion we never knew what to say or do. Now, only words we used normally on leaving the house would come.

'Ta-ta,' Big 'Ina said. 'Look after yerself.'

Yet we both knew this was such a great step, an even worse parting than being 'sent up the country' as an evacuee. When I heard my mother going to the front door, I dashed out of the kitchen, and gave her a tiny peck of a kiss. This really brought tears. We had never embraced before. It was a sloppy thing to do, unless with girls up a dark entry. But at that moment it seemed right, such a fitting end to my life in that small house, the heavenly world of our big brass bed where we all slept together. I listened to Big 'Ina making her way down the street, a sound for which I had waited so often as a child, late at night. It had meant security, the confirmation of our life. In adolescence, the same footsteps had often caused me annoyance. Yet in my chequered career since coming back from the country, there had been many times when I was pleased to be in our home again. I realized that now, over The Water, the footsteps would never be heard at all, either for good or bad.

When Big 'Ina had gone, and no further sound of her shoes could be caught, I went into the parlour to be alone and pray quietly, tearfully. But a child came and perched himself on the window-sill outside. I did not order him off, as I would have done once. I could not even recognize him. Perhaps he was one of those children, now grown older, whom my sisters once pushed around in prams to earn a stray penny. We had been better behaved as children, than to sit on somebody's parlour window-sill. The corner house was an exception, of course, because the sill there had always been used by the 'big fellas' as a grandstand. The song of our street was already dying. I must go.

The station presented a more auspicious sight. It was what a missionary could expect by way of a send-off. My farewell with Big 'Ina, all feeling and no outward show, was exactly reversed. But the evangelical friends who assembled on the platform were determined to demonstrate their solidarity. Separation from the 'world' was easily shown by forming a circle, and this was undertaken by Stanley. The soldiers hurrying past, loaded with kit, could not help but notice us. The hymns we sang managed to vie with the whistles and escaping steam. Prayers were less audible, but we did manage to fit in a few brisk testimonies, short shouted life histories of the before and after 'conversion' type. We probably hoped that some of the troops, cramming on to the boat-train, were going to fall on their knees and beg to be 'saved'. With the impossible packs and kitbags and rifles and gas-masks they carried, it was not surprising that our expectations went unsatisfied.

A disinterested observer must have found the whole situation unbelievable. A stream of khaki and blue, swearing and flustered, barged along the platform, struggling to get into the train and find a seat. Many would soon be pouring on to the Normandy beaches, snipping barbed-wire, trying to dodge German bullets or bombs. And there, in midstream, stood this odd collection of odd people, dressed gravely with grave expressions. They were apparently oblivious of the urgency around them. A second-hand dealer might have discovered them under a pile of Victorian junk, and have dumped them on the platform for sale. Could any cogs more incongruous than these be imagined in the war-machine's heart? Perhaps the knot of not-of-this-world people were a sign of surviving freedom.

I was transformed. This occasion of first wearing the college clothes certainly made me feel I could do justice to the role of departing martyr. I wore a new black jacket and striped trousers from Montague Burton. One hand held my umbrella and dark grey Anthony Eden hat, the other clutched my preacher's Bible-wallet. The collar of the new white shirt chafed my neck, and the rather pointed-toe, black shoes were decidedly less comfortable than the bare feet I had in the Fermanagh turf-bogs. Still, the call to battle could not be answered without the proper armour.

Anticipation tingled in my veins, and kept me from paying

attention to the final prayers and blessings being called down on me. Although my head was bowed, and my eyes apparently closed, I managed to peep at my watch, and counted the seconds that remained before departure. At last everyone agreed I ought to climb aboard. I stood at the door, my hand raised to the little group, exactly as I had seen famous people do on newsreels, in my 'worldly' days. I must have looked impressive, and made the poor dears feel that their efforts on my behalf were not wasted. Missionary I was, without doubt, even though my ration card might be a blue one, and my thoughts were not above but below, in fact, dwelling on the possible contents of the envelopes slipped into my pocket by the well-wishers. Then I went to the non-smoker, where I had kept a seat. Soldiers sprawled in the compartment, excited like myself. The prospect of being shipped like cattle, with the by no means uncertain possibility of slaughter at the other end, could not leave the most undemonstrative of beings unmoved. So they smoked in the non-smoker. Stanley was shocked by this. He pointed to the evil spirals rising all round me. A bolder elder came to the window and remonstrated with the offenders. Amongst other things, one of the soldiers told our brother to 'go to hell'.

Altercation abruptly ended at the whistle. My friends moved away and I left the window. I was glad to go. Though kind and well-meaning, my evangelical friends were apt to be unnecessarily obtuse on occasions. To upset the soldiers in the non-smoker struck me as pointless. From wanting to be the centre of the evangelical group, I now wanted to merge unnoticed in the horde of young men around me. Avoiding the non-smoker, I found another compartment. English airmen occupied this and not suspecting what sort of uniform my morning suit was, moved up to make room for me.

They had been stationed near Maggie's farm in Fermanagh.

Instead of doing my witness and handing out tracts as I should have done, I asked them how they liked the beautiful West. Yes it was fine if a little lonely at times, they said, but then you always knew people on farms where you went, as if it was your own home. And from this general picture, which immediately made me feel homesick, we went into detail, and found that one of the R.A.F. boys knew of Maggie, which made the homesickness worse. By talking about her, the very sound of her voice, the noise as she raked the fire at night, could be reconstructed. And what an extraordinary bond I felt with this 'unsaved' stranger, just because he remembered Maggie's farm vaguely. We laughed about the two red bags she carried on her bicycle handlebars. Lots of people knew her for she had to pass the R.A.F. camp on her way into town. The bags were actually two half-sacks which I had dyed red and put handles on. Maggie had thought them so 'posh', though they hung too low on her bicycle, and caused her many a tumble. With a qualm, I realized that Maggie and Christy too belonged, dreadfully, to the past. Just as there would be no more clopping of my mother's shoes over the pavement, so now I would not be able to jump a train to Fermanagh when crises arose. But I quickly dismissed the possibility of crises in my brand-new life.

In no time we reached Larne. We nudged our way to the boat through a mass of soldiers, who reminded me of cattle once more. It was Enniskillen fair day all over again when you could not move for beasts. Their rifles stuck in the air and got in the way, and made me think of cow-horns tossed impatiently above a sea of brown backs. I kept close to my airmen friends. They seemed quite used to this kind of crush, and knew how to work slowly forwards. Besides, they embodied the two things in life that meant most to me. Not only had they known my beloved Erne valley, where the most beautiful years of my life had been spent, but they also knew the marvels of England, where my immediate future lay. And like me, but long before me, these R.A.F. men were bound for far-away, exciting places, even if it was only to fight.

Because the crowd was almost exclusively male, Gertie looked most conspicuous.

I thought it must be somebody else. But on spotting me she came over, all smiles, to push a picnic basket into my hands, full of food for the journey. Nobody else had thought of that, not even the Little Lady, though it would take a day and night to travel from Scotland right down to the south of England. But I was too amazed at Gertie's presence to be grateful for her thoughtfulness, and for coming all the way to Larne. Not without shame, I realized that my surprise at Gertie's coming was, in fact, embarrassment. Try as I might the feeling would not go. At the farm she had seemed so radiant and attractive. But now in her best meeting-clothes she had an odd appearance, old-fashioned and stuffy—too much chiffon, too many artificial flowers, and her mother's Victorian brooches. Those clothes made her so much older-looking. One of the airmen asked if she were my mother.

Distress, rather than snobbery, made me short with her. I felt sorry for Gertie, having gone to so much trouble, only to meet with surliness that she must have noticed. And I felt angry with my own reaction to her suprise visit. I ought to have been overjoyed, that my departure was completed by a blessing from this last link with my past, with Ireland. But there I was, fuming inwardly. Perhaps the airmen's company affected me. Certainly had I been alone, a last few moments with Gertie would have given me joy. And had there been time, we might have wandered beyond the town, while I teased her about the un-smart clothes, until hat and scarves had been snatched off and stuffed in the bag.

Brutally wishing that she had not seen me, I became on edge again. I was terrified that she would want a parting prayer, there and then on the quayside. What would my fine airmen friends think of that? She was already talking rather loudly about 'journeying mercies' and 'uniting at the Throne'. I began to drop hints to Gertie that if she delayed leaving for home, she would be late in feeding the calves. Gertie showed no sign that she noticed my eagerness to be rid of her. Perhaps the cruel shafts caused some inner wound, which pride made her conceal. They may have been the kind of wound, that even time has difficulty in healing. At any rate, Gertie was brave to the end. She pulled a promise-box from her hand-bag. I had to read aloud both our choices, as she had left her glasses at home. Then she began enquiries about my luggage, was there much, was it heavy, what had I packed in it? But I knew what lay behind these questions, Gertie was dying to know if the ram's-horn inkwell was packed. Firmness was needed to control the situation, and instead of answering, I sent her off to get some chocolate. Fortunately I had almost got to the barrier when she came hurrying back again, noticeable by her awkward country gait. She gave me a whole month's ration of sweets. Our eyes met, flickered as though to rekindle a dead flame, and dropped again. Gertie gave me the saddest smile I think I have ever seen before or since. It lit her face like a wan ray of sunshine, falling over a wide landscape on a watery winter day. Then, as we reached the barrier, she turned and made off to the cloakroom.

I was too thrilled over going aboard the steamer, to worry about how much Gertie must be crying.

From my cabin-boy days, I knew how long it took to get ships out of harbour. Although I was safely on board now and leaning over the rail watching the preparation for sailing, I knew we would not leave at once. And in that time there still remained danger for me. I was afraid that my elder sister, or one of the great-aunts would cause trouble. They could easily persuade Big 'Ina to inform the police that I was travelling without her express permission. Of course, I had not *asked* my mother if I could go to England, but merely *told* her I was. Big 'Ina tried to understand my independence, even if it did not always please her. But other members of the family saw it as irresponsible high-handedness. As my mother's only son I had duties within the family, and more particularly in the shipyard. They resented my freedom from their clutches. Before the strip of water between boat and quayside widened, a policeman could wreck everything— 'Call', permit, training and 'field'. I could not help feeling as if I *ought* to be guilty, although my departure this time bore, literally, the stamp of official permission. It was like running away from the shipyard all over again.

But the engines throbbed through the ship, shaking it as purring shakes a cat. And we left without ceremony or fuss. Larne slipped away. So did the Antrim coast, the ring of sea-horizon gradually joined on itself. I tried to identify the fading coastline. Somewhere over there lay the cove—our cove with its annular ridges of seaweed and the smell of summer bodies.

A rush of nostalgia overwhelmed me then, and remorse for treating Gertie so badly. What hours we had spent on that little beach, far away now. The sea air sharpened my appetite and I opened her hamper. How beautifully everything was packed. I thought of her in the farm kitchen that morning, carefully preparing the basket, laying everything in place. The bread alone brought memories. I knew that never another griddle would bake such delicious golden-meal farls as did

Gertie's—just as mown hay on the sundown airs would never rise so sensuous or evocative as on that final walk with her to the spring-well. Now she would be on her way back to the farm, for the milking. Later, she would be giving the cats their supper in the sweet-smelling barn. By the time I got the train in Scotland she would take a last look in the hayshed, then the back door would be bolted for the night.

Satan was at work, I knew, in conjuring these pictures in my mind. But nevertheless, I did not take out my Bible to look up the texts Gertie had written on the hard-boiled eggs. Instead I cracked the shells, and threw them overboard. I watched them float down to the churning water. For a moment they rode the surface. Then the foam took them under.